NEW ERA VALUE INVESTING

RELATIVE VALUE DISCIPLINE

This book describes an innovative investment strategy called "Relative Value Discipline," which provides a framework for investing in traditional dividend-paying value stocks, as well as undervalued growth stocks. The graphic below illustrates how the stock selection process works step by step to winnow a thousand large cap stocks down to a focused portfolio of twenty to thirty holdings.

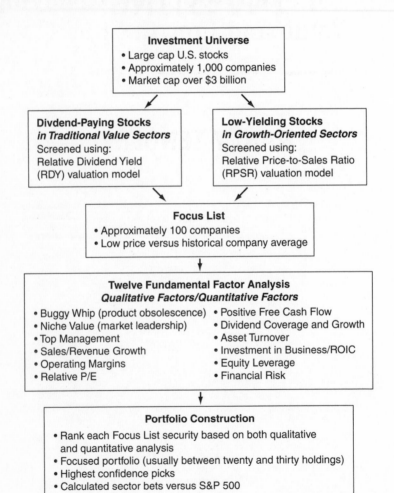

Investment Universe
- Large cap U.S. stocks
- Approximately 1,000 companies
- Market cap over $3 billion

Divdend-Paying Stocks
in Traditional Value Sectors
Screened using:
Relative Dividend Yield
(RDY) valuation model

Low-Yielding Stocks
in Growth-Oriented Sectors
Screened using:
Relative Price-to-Sales Ratio
(RPSR) valuation model

Focus List
- Approximately 100 companies
- Low price versus historical company average

Twelve Fundamental Factor Analysis
Qualitative Factors/Quantitative Factors
- Buggy Whip (product obsolescence)
- Niche Value (market leadership)
- Top Management
- Sales/Revenue Growth
- Operating Margins
- Relative P/E
- Positive Free Cash Flow
- Dividend Coverage and Growth
- Asset Turnover
- Investment in Business/ROIC
- Equity Leverage
- Financial Risk

Portfolio Construction
- Rank each Focus List security based on both qualitative and quantitative analysis
- Focused portfolio (usually between twenty and thirty holdings)
- Highest confidence picks
- Calculated sector bets versus S&P 500

NEW ERA
VALUE INVESTING
A Disciplined Approach to Buying
Value and Growth Stocks

NANCY TENGLER

WILEY

John Wiley & Sons, Inc.

Published by John Wiley & Sons, Inc., Hoboken, New Jersey
Published simultaneously in Canada

For general information on our other products and services, or technical support, please contact our Customer Care Department within the United States at 800-762-2974, outside the United States at 317-572-3993, or fax 317-572-4002.

Wiley also publishes its books in a variety of electronic formats. Some content that appears in print may not be available in electronic books.

Library of Congress Cataloging-in-Publication Data:

ISBN 0-471-26608-6

Printed in the United States of America
10 9 8 7 6 5 4 3 2 1

CONTENTS

PREFACE   ix

ACKNOWLEDGMENTS   xv

CHAPTER 1   Is It Really "Different" This Time?   1

CHAPTER 2   A Short History of Fundamental Analysis and the
Dividend   13

CHAPTER 3   The Development of Relative Dividend Yield   21

CHAPTER 4   The Challenges of the 1990s   33
An Historical View of U.S. Productivity   37

CHAPTER 5   The Twelve Fundamental Factors of RDY and RPSR
Research   51
Qualitative Appraisal   53
Quantitative Appraisal   61

CHAPTER 6   RDY Case Studies   85
Oil Stocks   86
Pharmaceutical Stocks   88
Classic Fallen-Angel Growth Stocks   90
Consumer Stocks   93
Bank Stocks/Financials   97
RDY Failures—Terminally Cheap Stocks   100

CHAPTER 7   RPSR Case Studies   105

RPSR and the Technology Bubble   106

The Intersection of RDY and RPSR   120

CHAPTER 8   Constructing a Value-Driven Portfolio   129

Merged Companies Combining High-Growth and Slow-Growth
Components   141

New Companies with Too Short a History   142

CHAPTER 9   What Is Value Investing Today?   145

**CHAPTER 10   Seven Critical Lessons We Have Learned as
Disciplined Investment Managers   153**

1. Wall Street Tends to Take Current Trends and Extrapolate Them
Out to Infinity.   154

2. It Is Rarely "Different This Time."   154

3. Market Workouts Are Often Great Investment
Opportunities.   156

4. At Turning Points, Go with Your Discipline—
Not Wall Street.   157

5. Investment Managers Need to Challenge Their Beliefs
Every Day.   161

6. Use the Availability of Data and the Always-On Financial Media
to Your Advantage.   162

7. It's All Relative.   162

APPENDIX A   New Era Value Composite   165

Disclosure   165

**APPENDIX B   Estee Lauder—Twelve Fundamental Factors:
Estee Lauder Companies, Inc. Valuation Factors   169**

Qualitative Appraisal   170

Quantitative Appraisal   173

APPENDIX C   EMC—Twelve Fundamental Factors: EMC Valuation Factors   181

    Qualitative Appraisal   182

    Quantitative Appraisal   189

APPENDIX D   Walt Disney—Twelve Fundamental Factors: The Walt Disney Company Valuation Factors   197

    Qualitative Appraisal   198

    Quantitative Appraisal   208

INDEX   215

PREFACE

Most books on equities investing are written during the advanced stages of bull markets when the public's interest in the subject is peaking. This book was written almost two and a half years into a wrenching bear market by a portfolio manager whose investment performance has not been particularly good in this exceptionally challenging market environment. This begs two questions: Why now? Why me?

The answer to the first query is easy. As a died-in-the-wool value investor, I believe in buying cheap and selling dear. Relatively few stocks are truly cheap during the latter stages of a bull market, whereas there are plenty of great fundamental bargains toward the end of a bear market. Bear markets are a perfect time for investors to pick off great companies at low valuations. What better time to introduce a value-driven investment discipline to investors?

The answer to the second query is a little trickier. I've spent my entire seventeen-year career as a value manager for large companies, municipalities, mutual funds, and individual investors. My quest for value has resulted in a focus on discipline both from a valuation and fundamental research standpoint. The Relative Price-to-Sales Ratio (RPSR) strategy detailed in this book has not been especially effective over the last eighteen months. Is this a cause for concern? We think not. The most important thing when employing a discipline is consistent implementation. RPSR has identified cheap high-quality companies, and the market will eventually follow. The discipline works because the market cycles; if investors remain constant it will come back our way. Relative Dividend Yield (RDY), our original valuation discipline, has produced results over the long term but has struggled during periods when growth investing ruled. But, by their very long-term nature, both strategies will identify stocks that will not outperform each and every year. However, they will outperform over the long term, which should be the time horizon of most investors. The disciplines this book will discuss have produced excellent long-term track records, which I believe will help readers target the stocks that will produce the most generous returns in the years ahead.

There has been a long-running debate on whether growth-at-a-reasonable-price methodologies such as mine qualify as value investing. This debate has intensified over the last year, as traditional value portfolios have outperformed and value-oriented growth stock investing has underperformed. Indeed, "absolute value" investors, with low price/earnings ratio portfolios concentrated in the most defensive market sectors, have had considerably more success than anyone else as the stock market has plummeted over the last few years, which is how it should be. I believe in traditional value stocks and hold some in my portfolios, but with the flexibility of the discipline this book will be introducing to you, I am able to identify stocks that trade at value-investor valuations, with growth-investor earnings potential. Coming out of a bear market, this is where investors want to be. Over the long term, I believe buying industry "Cadillacs" when the dealer (the market) is offering big incentives is a better definition of value than buying more cheaply priced, but much slower and poorer quality "Yugos." Put another way, "cheap" is not a synonym for "good value."

Warren Buffett, the most famous value investor of our time, is what I would call a growth-at-a-reasonable-price investor. Mr. Buffett has earned his well-deserved reputation as a connoisseur of value by buying high-quality growth companies when they are experiencing temporary difficulties or, for whatever reason, have lost favor in the market. Although over the short term, Mr. Buffett's portfolio of "fallen angel" growth stocks has periodically underperformed, over the long term they have made Berkshire Hathaway (Buffett's holding company) shareholders an enormous amount of money.

As I write (October, 2002), the Dow Jones Industrials and S&P 500 are at four-year lows and the NASDAQ Composite is off almost 77 percent from its March 2000 peak. Naturally, some commentary about this wrenching bear market is in order. At this stage, I think the most important thing to understand is that as investors approach bull market peaks and bear market bottoms, they develop an almost total disregard for fundamentals. Back in late 1999 and early 2000, investors didn't care about P/E ratios. They simply wanted to buy stocks because they were going up. Wall Street was bending over backwards to justify sky-high valuations and their nearly unanimous buy recommendations. Today, investors are equally oblivious to fundamentals. The S&P 500 is trading at about fifteen times next year's earnings estimates—near its historical P/E average and lower than one might expect given today's historically low bond yields and inflation, as well as improving economic and earnings trends. But investors seem to be ignoring the improvements, waiting for what they call visibility. This reflects doubt that earnings will be as good as anticipated.

Normally, low bond yields combined with relatively good economic and corporate earnings news would buoy the stock market. But not this time. The financial press and politicians gearing up for mid-term elections are placing most of the blame for the market's dismal performance this summer on the "crisis in confidence" spawned by accounting scandals and corporate malfeasance. This makes good copy and provides politicians airtime and ammunition to use against their opponents in the upcoming elections. However, the turmoil and volatility is likely to continue for some time. For times like these, the valuation disciplines are made to order.

In my view, one of the benefits of this bear market is that it has seasoned a whole generation of investors. Healthy fear and respect of the bear is a good thing and will result in prudent, intelligent investors. In our family of mutual funds, Fremont

Funds, individual investors have been doing exactly what they should be doing: averaging into a diversified portfolio of funds. Outflows have been modest.

I wrote this book because I believe passionately in the virtues of *discipline* in investing. If you find our valuation discipline of interest—great! If not, find a discipline that appeals to your appetite for risk and your long-term return objective. But whatever your investing profile, be disciplined. A consistently applied discipline will ensure success. I will leave you with two of my own experiences that illustrate why discipline is so important. The stories have been told before, to Allen Clarke for his book *Adventures in Investing*, but bear repeating because they illustrate the importance of investment discipline so perfectly.

> *Best Investment*: In the spring of 1999, Oracle Corporation became attractive on a valuation basis. According to the way we look at the world, the stock had rarely been cheaper. The market was discounting slowing growth in application software. But Oracle was focused on Internet computing and the trend away from personal computers to servers. Oracle's commitment was articulated best by founder and CEO Larry Ellison, who believed that the best way to demonstrate the value of the Internet to Oracle's customers was to become an Internet-centric company centered around their own products—a brilliant move that served not only to lower the company's operating expenses but also to stimulate demand for new Internet applications. Oracle proceeded to beat estimates and "wow" the Street. Of equal importance to us was the quality of management and the fact that Larry was "engaged" in the company once again. Using the Larry Ellison indicator has proven to be a successful way to buy the stock—it performs better when he is in charge and not so well when he is sailing around the world in his yacht. The results? We realized about a 600 percent return from our acquisition price.[1]

Oracle is a classic example of how RPSR can be used to profitably invest in value-oriented growth stocks.

Worst Investment: Ignoring one of my long-held tenets of never taking stock tips from friends, I did something worse: I took a stock tip from a stranger of sorts. He wasn't a strange stranger; after all, I met him in first-class on a cross-country flight. He was CFO of a company that was in the midst of an IPO road show. We didn't talk about the deal, but we did talk. And after the IPO I would watch the stock from time to time. It took off and produced exponential returns for the investment bankers and early investors. After about six months the stock pulled back about 50% and I jumped in, breaking all my own rules. I knew nothing about the fundamentals of the company beyond what business they were in and I knew nothing of the management except that the CFO was a very funny guy. I bought 200 shares of Smartalk Services (SMTK) for each of my kids' college accounts. "A little speculative growth can't hurt," I told myself. I purchased the stock at around $16 per share after an earnings disappointment. The first warning is rarely the last. The stock was eventually delisted and the company filed for bankruptcy. When I can get a value for my shares it shows a price of pennies per share.

I did just about everything wrong in that transaction, but the most critical error was buying stock in a company I knew nothing about. I didn't follow my discipline and I *gambled* with my hard-earned money. Although I will never salvage the loss, the shares remain in the account as a painful reminder of my error.[1]

NANCY TENGLER

NOTE

1. Allen Clarke, *Allen Clarke's ADVENTURES IN INVESTING, How to Create Wealth and Keep It* (Key Porter Books Limited 2000).

ACKNOWLEDGMENTS

The acknowledgements section of a book always reminds me of 8th grade graduation. The part where the principal stands up and tells the graduates that they will be sorely missed since "you are the best class to ever pass through these halls." Yeah, right.

The traditional *thanks to all who dedicated so much of their time to this manuscript* falls flat. I would like to raise the bar for all future authors who drain the time and intellect of so many to achieve so little.

First and foremost I want to thank the founding fathers of this great country for one of the most successful experiments in free trade and capitalism ever ventured. To all the investors who every day take their hard-earned money and invest in the future of this country and their own retirement while fighting the hangovers of insider trading and corporate accounting fraud and terrorist attacks and economic slowdown, you are the real heroes of capitalism—you have my enduring respect.

In the development of this tutorial on our approach to "skinning the cat" I would like to thank the beyond-the-call-of-duty efforts of Bill Fergusson and Michelle Swager of Fremont Investment Advisors. In addition to the creative demands and deadlines of running the marketing activities for a mutual fund complex, Bill and Michelle devoted hours of their personal time to fact-checking and editing this book. They made strategic contributions and added to the overall interest and editorial content of what you are about to read. In her spare time Michelle got married and Bill went to Fiji.

Steve Kindell assisted in developing much of the content in the book. Steve is an incredibly bright and lively contributor. After this mundane project, I recommend that Steve write the definitive history of the world—if anyone can do it, he can. His seemingly endless knowledge and turn of a phrase was a great help and was sincerely admired.

The analytical team at FIA should be awarded hazard pay for devoting enormous effort to navigating through a bear market and then having the annoyingly pesky task of responding to my requests for data . . . and more data. Harshal Shah, Joe Cuenco and Matt Costello provided historical perspective for the companies they cover and important analytical insight—not to mention all of the charts!

Noel DeDora and I have worked together since 1984. It's been a load of fun and Noel continues to be the single smartest individual I have ever met. (He is also the perfect straight man.) Noel has contributed a lot to my view of the world and my education of the capital markets. His early adaptation of RPSR as a way to identify value outside the dividend paying pool of stocks we had fished in for so many years was revolutionary at the time. After thirty years in the business, he has seen it all and made a ton of money for our clients. When he does decide to leave behind the "old stock and bond place" as he calls it, he will be greatly missed indeed. Luckily the investment business doesn't require heavy lifting, and I am hopeful he will remain involved for decades to come.

I would also like to extend my thanks to Ed Sporl, a well-regarded investment professional who graciously took the time to provide insight and factual confirmation for parts of the book. Dan Stepchew interned with us during the writing of this manuscript and was given the unending job of checking data of all sorts. Let's hope that experience has not deterred him from pursuing a career in the investment management business—we need fresh, young minds, Dan!

Deb McNeill and Cathy Smart added research elements that reflect their unique skills. Kathy Ribeiro assists me on a day-to-day basis with the business of running the business I oversee at Fremont Investment Advisors. If I could come back with the ideal disposition and attitude—it would be Kathy's. My sincere thanks to KR for keeping things moving in a calm and determined manner.

Many thanks to Nicole Young for the excellent advice she gave us as we embarked on this project, and for referring us to Gail Ross, whose services as lawyer and agent are much appreciated. And thanks to Bill Glasgall, Editorial Director of Investment Advisor magazine, for referring us to Jeanne Glasser, Senior Editor at John Wiley and Sons.

Jeanne Glasser has provided valuable direction and encouragement. Jeanne's vision to take an "out of the box" view of the world like the one outlined in this book is a tribute to the quality of the team at Wiley that continues to turn out interesting and thought-provoking financial books. I am very grateful for Jeanne's guidance and patience.

Lastly, I would like to thank my old friend, Al Krause, who had nothing directly to do with this book, but everything to do with bringing a constantly provocative view of the world that I find endearing, amusing, and personally challenging. Thanks for continuing to stoke the desire to learn and improve, Al.

NANCY TENGLER
2002

1

IS IT REALLY "DIFFERENT" THIS TIME?

"In Wall Street the only thing that's hard to explain is—next week."

Louis Rukeyser

"It's different this time" is a phrase impressionable young value investors are taught to challenge from the moment they decide to walk the value-investing path. As students of history and the markets know, any given situation is rarely "different this time." Value investors make a nice living for their clients and themselves by thoughtfully betting against those who say that it is difficult, if not impossible, to make money on stocks that are out of favor. For example, successful value investors were able to profit on oil stocks purchased in the early 1980s, after oil prices plunged from their late 1970s highs. They were able to profit on health care stocks when the Clinton Administration's failed attempts to reform health care in the early 1990s severely depressed equity valuations in the sector. And they were able to position themselves to later profit in defense stocks as investors during the mid- to late 1990s temporarily lost confidence in an industry undergoing wholesale consolidation after a period of severe cutbacks in defense spending.

But sometimes it *is* "different," and the astute investor can adapt and profit from changes in the market. This book chronicles the adaptation of a reluctant died-in-the-wool value investor to changes in the marketplace. It is about an investor who wholeheartedly believes the notion that it is rarely "different this time," but who knows that one has to move decisively when the world changes. It is about an investor who is loath to go with the Wall Street lemming crowd chasing after the thought of the moment, but who learned that, on select occasions, new approaches can make a good idea better.

At its roots, value investing is based upon the premise that it is possible to consistently find stocks that can be purchased at a discount to their true worth. The notion of value investing is made possible due to reliable valuation benchmarks that can be used to determine the true worth of any security, and the belief that these benchmarks remain relatively stable despite fluctuations in a stock's price. Value investors are constantly evaluating how to consistently apply this premise to a changing investment environment.

Sound money management derives as much from the ability to follow a discipline as it does from the skills of the money manager. Investing is always tinged with emotion. There are any number of reasons to fall in love with a stock and remain committed to it long after it ceases to be a good investment. Every money manager, no matter how disciplined, has owned such stocks. Likewise, a stock that has fallen out of favor can be a true bargain yet be ignored because an investor has come to regard the stock and the company with extreme wariness. For this reason, discipline is valuable (in fact, essential). Discipline helps to anchor an investor by taking the emotion out of the buy or sell decision. A well-conceived investment discipline focuses investors in areas they would otherwise avoid if they were following the Wall Street herd mentality. Likewise, a properly formulated investment discipline should provide clear and well-defined sell signals to avoid the inevitable "roundtrip" so many investors experience. The use of structures, tools, and formulas that can provide a consistent return on investment is fundamental to a money manager's process. This is particularly important in a market prone to cyclical changes, which can cause managers to doubt their investment processes and become victims of their own emotions. As Figure 1.1 illustrates, investment approaches come in and out of favor, and when the discipline followed is not in favor, it can be tempting to shift with the changes in fashion. Every investment manager has had occasion to question his or her investment approach during these times of stress. But one thing is certain—when you just can't take it anymore, it's time to double down your bet if your discipline is sound.

A well-thought-out investment discipline can perform satisfactorily for a very long time because the markets are cyclical and history is a good teacher. However, rapid shifts in the structural components of the economy and in the character of the securities markets can sometimes limit some disciplines that had previously worked well. When a long-standing discipline

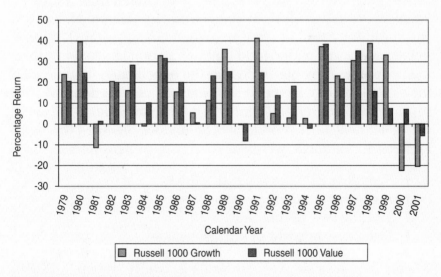

Figure 1.1   Russell 1000 Growth vs. Russell 1000 Value, 1979–2001
Source: Data from Frank Russell Company.

no longer provides a manager with a sufficient number of strong choices from which to build a diversified portfolio, or eliminates healthy companies in favor of others that are not, the manager is forced to re-examine his or her discipline to determine if it is still relevant on the whole or whether adjustments may be called for. Revising an investment discipline should never be undertaken lightly, however, because discipline is a key element in keeping managers true to their investment mandates. At turning points in the market, managers tend to question their disciplines, which is usually the point when one needs to remain most devoted to it. Zigging when one should zag is an expensive lesson to learn, as it is often deleterious to the value of a portfolio. Changing disciplines can be a sure way to lock in recent underperformance compounded by the loss of outperformance about to come your way.

In looking at value investing in today's market, it is important to understand the historical roots from which it originated. Value investing as a method for selecting stocks was created by Benjamin Graham and David Dodd in the late 1920s and early 1930s, and released in their 1934 work, *Security Analysis*. Value investing as described by Graham and Dodd worked extraordinarily well at the time. When Graham and Dodd first published, it was understood that not all stocks would fit their methodology. They observed that the benchmarks that defined their methodology included the payment of a regular dividend (even in the 1920s and 1930s, there were many stocks that never paid a dividend). Their original benchmarks, based on Graham's lectures at Columbia, were:

I Five-year EPS growth rate < 7.5 percent
I Five-year dividend growth rate > 0
I Trailing twelve-month EPS > 0
I Price < 80 percent of intrinsic value

where the intrinsic value = Trailing twelve months EPS × $(8.5 + (2 \times 5 - \text{year EPS growth rate}) \times (4.4/\text{AAA corporate bond yield}))$.

As shown by the equations, the dividend is a necessary component of this methodology. Graham determined, through observation and an extensive examination of historical records, that once a stock fits the basic criteria there was a fairly constant ratio between earnings growth and the price/earnings ratio (P/E), which could be expressed in a formula:

$$P/E = 8.5 + (2 \times \text{growth}), \text{ or}$$
$$\text{Price} = \text{Earnings} \times (8.5 + (2 \times \text{growth}))$$

In the 1970s Graham enlarged his rule set to ten rules, in order to take into account Net Current Asset Value, the current assets of a company minus all of its liabilities. In 1984, as a validation of the Graham and Dodd approach, Henry Oppenheimer published a study of the revised selection criteria in the *Financial Analysts Journal.* Using various groupings of the criteria over the period from 1974 to 1981, he determined that certain groups gave truly outstanding performance, but that the overall group consistently outperformed basic benchmarks.

THE BIRTH OF GRAHAM AND DODD INVESTING

It is worth noting exactly why Graham and Dodd's book was first written. You may remember that even the best money managers often question their disciplines. Benjamin Graham was just such a money manager. When Benjamin Graham graduated from Columbia College, he was considered such a promising scholar that he was offered teaching positions in English, mathematics, and philosophy. But he had already begun a career on Wall Street, working for Newburger, Henderson and Loeb, and by 1919 he was making a good living. In 1926 Graham formed an investment partnership to take advantage of the then-booming stock market. Despite his superior knowledge, he was ruined in the stock market crash. Graham took up teaching night classes in finance at Columbia to make ends meet, where he began to think about developing a more conservative investment methodology that would allow investors to weather future crashes. His lectures on the subject, transcribed by another Columbia professor, David Dodd, formed the basis of the book the two published.

The model Graham and Dodd developed is considered most useful for evaluating stocks that are large, grow at a slow but constant rate, and provide a large margin of safety for investors, partially through the payment of dividends. For stocks identified by this model, the total return, which is the growth rate of the stock plus the dividend yield, is said to provide an adequate and sometimes even substantial reward to patient investors with a high margin of safety. The Graham and Dodd method, as originally created, worked well on the shares of regulated public utilities, life insurance companies, food processing firms, medical supply companies, beverage makers, and household product companies. These were all companies that piled up sufficiently large amounts of cash, or had sufficient and constant earnings growth, that they could guarantee a steady dividend in good times and bad.

Consider that list for a moment. Regulated utilities—electricity generators, water companies, and the telephone company until deregulation—were all provided with a guaranteed rate of return on invested capital by their regulators in return for a steady commitment to new investment. This regulated rate of return always provided a strong enough surplus to ensure that the companies could pay a steady dividend. The same was true for life insurance companies, which needed to maintain large invested surpluses so they could pay off policyholders at the time of death, or if people cashed in or borrowed against their policies. Medical supply companies, food processing firms, household product companies, and beverage firms will sometimes grow faster than the rise in population, because of the introduction of new products or changing tastes, but they rarely grow slower than the rate of population growth. This allows them to engage in very long planning cycles, and requires them to maintain capital for ongoing investment. The surpluses from that capital, plus earned profits, are available for the payment of dividends.

While the Graham and Dodd model worked extremely well for more than forty years, by the 1980s, as the market continued to evolve, the absolute dividend criteria of the Graham and Dodd valuation model began to limit the investable universe of stocks as yields across the board declined. In the 1980s, many companies found that the large amounts of cash they carried made them vulnerable to takeovers. "Extra" dividends were in some cases used to get surplus cash off the balance sheet. In other cases, dividend cuts increased as managements attempted to free up cash, for reinvestment or as a reflection of what they determined to be the long-term sustainable earnings power of the company. These changes in the economy prompted the use of Relative Dividend Yield (the subject of Chapter 3) as a valuation metric when most value investors were looking at P/E ratios or absolute yield to define cheapness.

After the disappointing 1970s and the slow growth of the early 1980s, another change gradually developed in the economy. The root cause of this change was an unprecedented increase in productivity attributable to the use of technology, including computers and, later, the Internet. These improvements enabled the United States to experience a prolonged period of sustainable, non-inflationary growth. With this came a corporate focus on growth, and the dividend became less relevant. At the time of this writing the trend continued despite the correction of an overexuberant market, and experts believed that as long as inflation stays in check, the trend will continue with a profound impact on the economy and corporate America for the foreseeable future.

By the mid-1990s, this growth-oriented economy left money managers who followed dividend-driven disciplines with few choices. We had already adopted Relative Dividend Yield as an investment discipline but even with the "relative" component we were having difficulty finding enough attractive ideas. There had to be another way to identify value in companies that paid little or no dividends without returning to the earnings-estimate-driven P/E roulette of previous generations of value investors. An attractive alternative was needed to broaden the definition of what value investing was or could be, in order to expand the number of good, healthy companies in which it was permissible to invest. Ultimately, in response to a dynamic market, that is what we did. The decision to look at potential extensions of value investing in the mid-1990s had two major underpinnings:

1. **Classic valuation models were limiting the investable universe to dividend-paying companies**. In an economy dominated by dividend-paying companies, traditional value-investing approaches yielded ample investment opportunities. The economy of the 1990s saw a rapid rise in the growth-oriented technology, health care, and communications sectors, where a premium was paid for earnings growth that resulted in the appreciation of the underlying stock. Dividends (an upfront return payment) were no longer prized. Share buy-backs to fund options programs were increasing and the markets were rewarding companies with an ever-increasing focus on productivity. Value investors who adhered to their discipline were challenged to build diversified portfolios, particularly if the dividend was part of their valuation criteria. Many value hedge funds closed, value fund managers were fired, and others were treated like pariahs by the media (or worse yet, their clients). "Old" value portfolios just didn't deliver returns any more. In addition, as shown in Figure 1.2, in the mid- to late 1990s, the market experienced a tremendous shift in sector concentration to technology, health care, and communications, which were dominated by low or no dividend

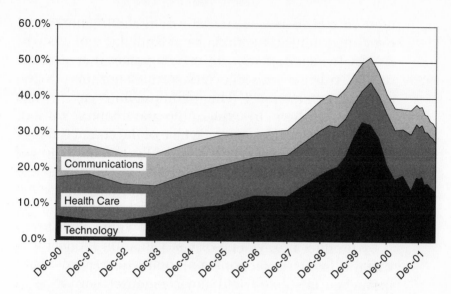

Figure 1.2 S&P 500 Sector Weightings December, 1990 to September, 2002
Source: Data from Vestek.

stocks—hardly the stomping ground of traditional value managers badly in need of generating attractive returns.

2. **In particular, value investors were being excluded from investing in some of the more innovative sectors of the market (e.g., technology) and a significant portion of the S&P 500.** As technology, health care, and telecommunications increased in weighting vis-à-vis the S&P 500, the value investor faced a real dilemma. It ultimately wasn't the relative performance drag that provided the biggest challenge to value investors but rather the lack of diversified, attractively valued companies. With less than 50 percent of the index available for value investing at the peak of the technology boom, what was the appropriate benchmark? When the Dow Jones Industrial Average added Intel and Microsoft to the index in 1999, value investors lost their last relevant index to benchmark against. A valuation

methodology was needed that would identify periods of over- and undervaluation for a broader universe of stocks, focusing specifically on companies that paid low or no dividends but still cycled through periods of over- and undervaluations. The paradox inherent in this search was how to widen the parameters without appreciably widening the risk. One of the characteristics of value investing is that it typically results in lower risk. (That relationship broke down in the 1990s, the first time in recent memory when traditional value portfolios underperformed in a down market, resulting in increased risk profiles for many value investors.) A by-product of dividend-driven valuation models was that the dividend component of total return (particularly in higher absolute yield environments) served as a damper to volatility. The investor at least earns a dividend while waiting for the stock to appreciate—he or she gets paid to wait. But in a growth (non-dividend-paying) biased market, what is the investor's reward for waiting patiently for price appreciation? Higher volatility. So our challenge was to develop an approach that we recognized would have inherently higher volatility, but not exceedingly so.

To step back for a moment, it is important when thinking about value investing disciplines to ensure one remains true to the underlying tenets of the approach. It is too easy to get wrapped up in "value" or "growth" investing as a set of definitions rather than as a set of structures and a discipline. As mutual funds began to proliferate during the 1980s, the issue of fund nomenclature began to cloud the minds of investors. Because value investing took root early, other disciplines looked to describe themselves in different ways. This may sound like a trivial matter, but it is not. Mutual funds are required to define their investment objectives and methods for their investors, and are held to their definitions in the construction of their portfolios.

Portfolios are also comparatively ranked within categories, so that potential investors may know what they are purchasing. For many fund managers, value investing means a discipline that in some way depends upon the payment of dividends as an evaluation tool, so that it becomes difficult to look beyond that and still be able to legitimately call yourself a value investor.

From my perspective, and the perspective of other colleagues, traditional dividend-driven value investing needed to be paired with a fresh approach that would allow investors to take advantage of the changes in the market while still not changing or compromising the underlying fundamentals of value investing. It was important to find a way to apply the disciplines inherent in value investing to a dynamic stock market. In my early years of investing, we adopted Relative Dividend Yield, which provided a good comparative tool for evaluating dividend-paying stocks. Now we were looking to extend value investing further into the realm of non-dividend paying stocks, which led us to create a new strategy called Relative Value Discipline, the focus of this book.

2

A SHORT HISTORY OF FUNDAMENTAL ANALYSIS AND THE DIVIDEND

"A study of economics usually reveals that the best time to buy anything is last year."

Marty Allen

My career as a value investor began in the mid-1980s. At that time the concept of value investing was already fifty years old. The value discipline that I worked with then was several steps removed from the discipline described by Graham and Dodd in their 1934 book, *Security Analysis*. The discipline that I use now is quite different from the one that I used two decades ago.

This evolution occurred because markets are not static. Although you will see that I believe that the markets do not go through major evolutions on a short-term basis,[1]—it is rarely different this time—the markets have undergone a slow evolution since the early 1990s. For example, markets have become more transparent as technology has made financial data more available. Investment managers have had to adjust their investment strategies to take advantage of increasing levels of information. To understand how value disciplines have changed, it is instructive to look at the evolving roles of both fundamental analysis and the dividend.

Broadly speaking, value investing can be thought of as a disciplined process for identifying and investing in undervalued stocks with strong upside potential. Today there is a broad spectrum of disciplines that fall under the value umbrella, each attributable to investment managers attempting to respond to current market conditions. Well-known value investors ranging from Warren Buffet to Michael Price to Mario Gabelli each take a unique approach to value investing.

Graham and Dodd's *Security Analysis* created the discipline of pairing quantitative screens with fundamental analysis that would lay the groundwork for the subsequent development of Relative Dividend Yield, or RDY (which is discussed in Chapter 3). My own investment discipline, Relative Value Discipline, is an outgrowth of RDY which extends relative value investing to low and non-dividend paying companies through the use of Relative Price-to-Sales Ratio. Central to the methodology of all three are fundamental analysis and the dividend. Graham and Dodd formalized an intellectual process that leads directly to Relative Value Discipline. They were part of an intellectual heritage that extends even further back in time, to two financial figures of the early twentieth century who are less-well-remembered today.

From today's perspective we would consider the stock markets of the late 1800s a gambler's paradise. Fraud and manipulation were the order of the day. Insiders had all the advantages over the average investor because there were few, if any, securities laws, as we know them, and very little reliable and accurate financial information on companies. Most businesses did not publish financial statements, and those that did often published statements that were misleading.

Two New Yorkers, Louis Guenther and Alfred Best, did a lot to change this situation. In 1902, Guenther released the first edition of *The Financial World*. This was a pocket-sized magazine, written in a journalistic style, that reported on and exposed securities fraud. Because it became wildly popular, this publication forced many companies to start reporting accurate information about their financial condition and their profitability. It also started a trend that eventually led to the enshrining of Guenther's concepts of fairness and accuracy in financial reporting in the securities laws enacted in the early 1930s.

Just a few years before the launch of *The Financial World*, Alfred Best began publishing a service, still in use today, that focused on the insurance industry. Best had the idea that by providing accurate financial data on fire insurance companies, not only would insurance buyers benefit, but so, too, would investors in insurance stocks. Later in his career on September 23, 1923, he completed his first analysis of fire insurance company stocks. In it, Best compared his estimate of what he called the *intrinsic value* of each stock to its then-current price. He wrote that:

> Some stocks were being sold above their intrinsic values, but in most cases the reverse was true; the price at which certain stocks could be bought being far below their worth at that time.

Best then went on to explain why these stocks were good investments:

> Insurance is one of the oldest and largest businesses in the world. American insurance companies engaged in the business of fire insurance are built on a solid foundation. Their development has gone hand in hand with the growth of the nation's wealth. The stockholders of such companies have seen the value of their holdings increase year after year while enjoying regular and increasing *dividends* (emphasis added). Fire insurance companies have no seasonal or fluctuating demands for their services and their business is relatively stable and constant. Although somewhat affected by economic conditions, the companies are not subject to severe losses as a result of panics or depressions. Consequently, insurance stocks are less subject to fluctuations than most other classes of market investments.[2]

Best's method of finding the intrinsic value of a stock became widely followed. Some analysts eventually began to think of applying his approach to the analysis of other kinds of companies as well. What worked for insurance companies could also work for other financial institutions (such as banks, for example) and for industrial firms (such as steel manufacturers). Best's idea—that a stock selling below its true value is a good investment—became more and more influential.

When Graham and Dodd's *Security Analysis* came out in 1934, it formalized the concept of intrinsic value and became the bible for fundamental stock analysis. It was the first work that spelled out a systematic method for using financial and market information to place a value on a company and to make a determination about whether or not its stock, at a certain price, was worth buying. This book remains the intellectual foundation of the profession of securities analysis, and its concepts, though evolved, are still in use today.

Benjamin Graham continued to modify his value-investing yardsticks (quantitative screens) in later years as the markets and the economy evolved, but he always stuck to his basic premise, namely, that selecting stocks through select quantitative screens (including a dividend related screen) and fundamental analysis paid off in better returns and less risk for investors.

Over the next forty years, however, the concept of value investing underwent many changes. The methods that had worked during the Great Depression needed to be updated for the period after World War II. Wartime production and deficit financing pulled the U.S. economy out of the 1930s doldrums, but, after the war, it produced periods of inflation and one business and stock market cycle after another that lasted well into the 1980s.

Business finance in the United States changed relatively little from the 1930s to the 1970s. When companies needed to expand, they borrowed the money from a bank or financed it out of retained earnings. If management chose the latter option, they would typically do it in a way that would not affect the dividend. Maintaining the dividend was sacrosanct. Corporate boards took their commitments to their dividend policies very seriously.

During the inflationary bubble and general malaise of the early 1970s, many American companies had difficulty in producing a predictable, growing stream of earnings although they did remain focused on paying a steady dividend. Only in a handful of companies, the so-called Nifty Fifty—postwar technology companies such as IBM, Xerox, and Polaroid, and conglomerates such as LTV—were top- and bottom-line growth achieved with the desired constancy. Because there were only a handful of firms that seemed capable of real growth, money poured into Nifty Fifty stocks, so much so that they became greatly overvalued. The bear market of 1973–1974 put an end to this mania, but inflation (and ultimately stagflation) continued to be a problem into the late 1970s.

Into this arena came a few intrepid investors who were destined to become legendary. Among them, Warren Buffett saw that many stocks had become seriously undervalued and took advantage of some incredible opportunities. In the early 1980s, many great companies were selling for very low multiples of earnings. What is more, half the stocks listed on the New York Stock Exchange were selling at a discount to their book values. Many were sound financially and had paid dividends consistently for years. Clearly they represented extraordinary values. Buffett saw this opportunity and became famous, as well as very rich. Buffett did this, for example, by buying into the likes of Coca-Cola and *The Washington Post* at ridiculously low prices. Buffett understood the meaning of value.

While many investors were content to allow market forces to drive the price of stocks upward, a number of individuals attempted to accelerate the pace, and in so doing forced a change in the fundamentals of the value-investing discipline. Mike Milken, T. Boone Pickens, Carl Icahn, and the investment banks they partnered with all served notice in the mid-1980s that American business could no longer go on as usual. Any company that had a large amount of cash on its balance sheet and underutilized plant and equipment was ripe for these corporate raiders, who forced a wave of consolidation in the oil, newspaper, communications, and airline industries that is still not complete even today. Corporate boards reacted with the payment of special dividends to shareholders to dispense their excess cash, or with acquisitions of their own that would soak up cash and allow companies to rationalize their resources and markets.

All of this led to a dramatic change in the market. By the mid-1980s, the dividend was no longer what it had been. Where it was once a solid measure of corporate accomplishment and a reward for patient investors, by the mid-1980s dividends had become, for many companies, a sign that the board had no better use for corporate cash than to give it back to shareholders. While followers of the traditional value discipline looked upon dividends as a sign of stability, others saw in dividends all the marks of stagnation. As the decade of the 1980s wore on, it was becoming increasingly difficult to make money for clients using a strict Benjamin Graham value methodology. This was certainly true of the methodology described in the first edition of *Security Analysis* and in Graham's original lectures, but also applied to the much-evolved, updated fifth edition of Graham's *The Intelligent Investor*, published in 1973. The market was changing, the role of the dividend was changing, and clearly value investing would have to change as well. For dividend-focused value investors, more challenges were yet to come.[3]

NOTES

1. A good example of a short-term change that appeared to be permanent was banking in the early 1990s. At that time many people were saying that traditional banking was "dead," but later saw that this was not true.

2. *Best Insurance Report*, September 20, 1923.

3. For a short discussion of how Graham changed his methodology over time see John Quirt, "Benjamin Graham: The Grandfather of Investment Value Is Still Concerned," in Janet Lowe, *The Rediscovered Benjamin Graham* (New York: John Wiley & Sons, Inc., 1999).

3

THE DEVELOPMENT OF RELATIVE DIVIDEND YIELD

"You try to be greedy when others are fearful, and fearful when others are greedy."

Warren Buffett

After the Nifty Fifty bull market and its subsequent decline in the early 1970s, wary investors were determined to establish valuation metrics and targets for the stocks in their portfolios. Investors swore that they would never again get sucked into the type of heady momentum market that had driven stock prices ever higher, leading to more and more optimistic forecasts for the future. Those days were over. Investors learned their lesson in the routing of the 1973–1974 bear market. Discipline was needed; discipline, and attention to valuation.

In the 1970s, long before technology made access to data available to professional and individual investors at the touch of a mouse, data was difficult to obtain. Professional analysts had to dig to find data and then required hours with a slide rule to calculate it into the desired ratio. Technology gradually improved and more and more data became available. Wall Street firms began to look in-depth at multiple financial characteristics when analyzing stocks. In the quest for discipline, valuation mattered and investors were willing to consider a variety of financial characteristics to identify cheap valuations. By the late 1970s, a few firms began to look at the historical *relative* yields of specific stocks and industries to build perspective on valuation. The perspective gained from looking at stocks compared to their own history, and compared to the market, was compelling. In the early 1980s, Roger Newell and Tony Spare, later my colleagues at the Bank of California, adopted Relative Dividend Yield (RDY) as a way of identifying when stocks were cheap and when they were expensive. In adopting this approach they understood that relative information was going to be more valuable over time than absolutes (see Chapter 4, page 42, and Chapter 10, page 162, for additional discussions on relative versus absolute measures). They were also interested in relative yield for the contribution to total return provided by consistent and growing dividends. The market yields were much higher then and a portfolio with an above-market yield could expect to receive half of its total return from the dividend.

The gradual development and adoption of new investment approaches is not a new story. Investment managers have always continued to search for new ways to profitably and reliably invest in the market, a search that continues to this day. However, the danger in this effort lies in the potential for constantly changing an investment approach depending upon the market of the day. There is a fine line between being completely open to new ideas and being fashionable, or driven by the trend of the moment. We have often said that having *any* investment discipline is good. Having a good discipline is better. Trend following is a surefire way to lose money . . . lots of it. Over the years, many portfolio managers and their clients have given up on their investment strategy at just the wrong time. The compounding effect of chasing the in-vogue strategy after it has already worked and abandoning the strategy that is about to work is quite costly. Sticking with any strategy will pay off over time. Chasing trends is a poor man's game.

At the time RDY was first adopted, we managed money for wealthy individuals in the bank's trust department of the Bank of California. Many of these individuals were in need of income; therefore, the logic of using a methodology around dividend yield was obvious. In the beginning we did not understand the compelling features of the discipline that we came to appreciate in later years, but Newell and Spare did find the relative yield discipline to be an effective way of buying and selling stocks for the *income equity* collective funds they ran at the bank. By the time I became involved in the management of the strategy, we were expanding our client base to demanding institutional, pension clients. The challenging questions and rigorous review process helped us evolve our thinking and crystallize our strategy as we bought and sold stocks using RDY. RDY was not an original concept; the *use* of RDY as a valuation discipline for stock selection was.

Before going into the details of what RDY is, it is important to look at why it works. RDY avoids relying on earnings, which are cyclical and at times difficult to predict, particularly at turning points. Dividends, however, don't require forecasting for the discipline to work. Further, the discipline reflects the policy of the corporate boards. Over time, we learned through our implementation of the RDY investing strategy, that the dividend was a good indicator of a company's own expectations of future earnings growth prospects and its overall business stability. We learned that the companies we were investing in tended to have *"dividend-paying cultures."*

The fact is, most dividend-paying companies do not slash their dividends haphazardly in response to market conditions. The reliability of the dividend policy is what helps to make RDY a stable valuation benchmark. Company boards pay close attention to their long-term cash needs, as well as to the capital needs of the company and the economic conditions. They set their dividend policies so that the dividend can remain a relatively constant percentage of earnings in good

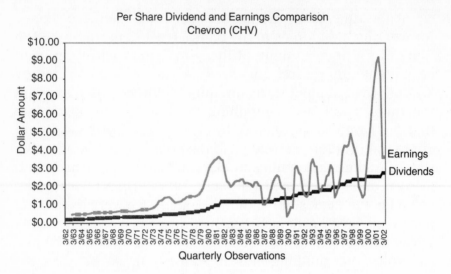

Figure 3.1 Per Share Dividend and Earnings Comparison Chevron (CHV)
Source: Data from Compustat.

times and bad. For example, when oil prices skyrocketed in the mid-1970s, the oil companies did not greatly increase their dividends. Nor did they sharply cut their dividends when prices and profits plummeted about a decade later. Figure 3.1 shows that, although Chevron's earnings have gyrated over time, the dividend has remained stable, growing at a slow deliberate pace. As such, it is a proxy for long-term sustainable earnings power, and a powerful indicator for investors.

A stable dividend policy provides reliable information about how corporate management views the firm's prospects for long-term earnings, as well as an income stream that is important to investors. The predictability of the income stream can be beneficial to investors, particularly in periods when the market is declining for longer than a few months, such as prolonged recessions.

PERSPECTIVE ON TRENDS IN THE 1980s MARKETS

The 1980s were actually a time of great intellectual ferment in the financial services industry. With the U.S. economy becoming genuinely competitive for the first time in over two generations, professional investors on Wall Street were all searching for tools that would provide consistent above-average returns while minimizing risk. Just as in the industrial economy, there was sudden competition, in this case for the new flood of money coming into the market from individual retirement accounts, corporate pensions, and later, 401(k) retirement plans. Small mutual fund firms such as Fidelity, which had been around since the 1920s, suddenly realized that a successful investment philosophy was also a successful marketing tool that could and did attract billions of dollars. Moreover, the introduction of low-cost computer memory and increasing processor speeds made it possible for investment managers to explore a variety of relationships among different financial factors to seek out those factors that would produce a set of reliable investment indicators. The investment markets in the 1980s represented a period when information technology, at least in the beginning, led to a large increase in productivity among investment managers, who could use better data to make better decisions.

Two additional technological factors impacting the changing investment climate of the 1980s were the development of a variety of investing algorithms that allowed trading to be automated to a certain extent, and advances in communication that enabled firms with their own proprietary telecommunications networks to gain an edge in getting the best price in trading. In the late 1980s, all of these forces came together at a number of firms to create so-called "black box" trading strategies, which were algorithmically driven opportunistic trades made on an automated basis, often by a supercomputer.

Another driver of change in the way investments were made was the development of more complex portfolio management tools. Until the 1980s, investors simply did not have the tools to compare the relative values not only of individual stocks, but of combinations of stocks in portfolios. Advanced portfolio analysis came of age during this period and provided money managers with an entirely new set of modeling tools.

Over time we found that RDY was a simple and useful methodology that allowed a comparison of the yield of any given stock to the yield of the market and to its own historical yield at any given time. As we wrote in 1992, when Tony Spare and I co-authored *Relative Dividend Yield: Common Stock Investing for Income and Appreciation,* "RDY allows the investor to identify stocks for purchase whose yield has risen relative to the market and to the stocks' own histories, as well as to determine when these stocks become overvalued by watching the key points at which the relative yield falls and the price increases."[1] With RDY we could know with great precision whether a given stock was overvalued or undervalued relative to others in its class, and whether it was overvalued or undervalued at that moment relative to the market as a whole and relative to its own history.

Relative Dividend Yield is a simple calculation and is established as follows (also see Figure 3.2 for a Relative Dividend Yield chart):

Yield = Indicated annual dividend rate/Current stock price

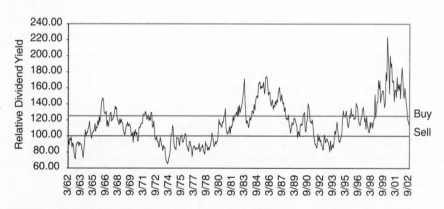

Figure 3.2   Company XYZ Relative Dividend Yield
Source: Data from Compustat.

Market index dividend yield = Indicated index annual
dividend rate/Current market value

Relative dividend yield (RDY) = Stock yield/Market index yield

Once this calculation is made, it is possible to repeat the calculation over time, in order to trace the rise and fall of yield relative to a market index. By doing this, an investor can identify potential opportunities for acquiring a stock. When RDY is high, this is an indication of undervaluation. When the RDY is low, it is an indication that the valuation is high, and that it is time to sell; or that the market is overvaluing an improvement in fundamentals; *or* that a stock has returned to favored "growth stock" status among analysts.

Figure 3.3 shows how the RDY methodology can be used to evaluate the attractiveness of a dividend-paying stock (for example, Coca-Cola). The buy range lies above the higher of the two horizontal lines; the sell range lies below the lower of the two lines. When a stock's RDY plots above the buy line, it is a candidate for purchase. When it moves below the sell line, it is a candidate for sale.

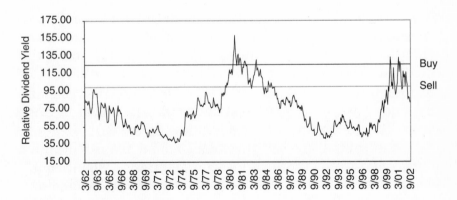

Figure 3.3 Coca-Cola (KO) Relative Dividend Yield
Source: Data from Compustat.

RDY CHARTS FOR FALLEN ANGELS

Coca-Cola (Coke) is a good example of how RDY can be used to invest in fallen-angel growth stocks. Figure 3.3 shows that Coke generally trades at a below-market yield and that the RDY investor has not been presented with many opportunities to buy the stock. If the fundamentals hold up when a fallen angel like Coke enters the buy range, it generally presents a tremendous investment opportunity. See Chapter 9 for a further discussion of Coke and Chapter 7 for other fallen angels.

To set the thresholds for buy and sell ranges, each stock is evaluated individually and its range established based on the stock's unique history. Two absolute parameters govern the range-setting process:

1. A stock can never be a candidate for purchase with an RDY of less than 125 percent; and

2. A default sell range is established when the stock yield drops to that of the market.

These parameters, supported by our own research, are necessary because dividends lose some of their significance when a stock has a below-market yield. In this case the dividend generally does not reflect management's view of the long-term earnings power of the company—the company does not have a "dividend-paying" culture, which is critical to the successful implementation of an RDY strategy. Once the ranges are set, the management team will move them only if the company's characteristics significantly change—for instance, because of merger and acquisition activity, material changes in the growth rate, or the sale of a significant area of the company's business which affect the company's profile.

We have found that RDY is an almost perfect negative sentiment indicator. When the RDY calculation signals that it is time to buy, it is really signaling that investors have so shunned/neglected a stock that they are demanding a huge upfront payment for the uncertain future value of the company. By pushing the stock price down until the dividend yield rises, investors note their displeasure or discouragement with management or a company's prospects relative to its competitors. In some ways, RDY makes stocks act more like bonds, where investors know that yields are the reciprocal of risk.

One of the problems with stocks that reach the RDY "buy" range is that, generally, no analyst will recommend them. The farther they go into the buy zone, the more likely this is to be true. That makes investors who use the RDY method look like true contrarians, because they are not simply purchasing stocks that are out of favor with Wall Street, but rather, stocks that Wall Street has deserted altogether. RDY offers a disciplined approach to investing and provides a disciplined approach to finding stocks when nobody else is looking for them.

It is not that we are merely contrarians, but rather, like any true value investors, we are always looking to exploit information gaps in the marketplace. Often the biggest gaps are in stocks that Wall Street has given up on. When analysts stop following a company, and when institutions desert it by selling the company's stock out of their portfolio, a company can have several good quarters, and sometimes several good years, without anyone noticing. We call this a "loss of constituency." A typical scenario would be a growth company like Coke or Johnson & Johnson that goes through a transition and is deserted by growth investors, but has not been discovered by value investors. The pharmaceuticals and consumer products companies each saw a mass exodus by growth managers in the early 1990s and late 1990s respectively. The stocks languished until value managers (a new constituency) got interested and prices began to rise.

Johnson & Johnson (JNJ) was another example of such a company—a former growth stock that lost the growth stock investor constituency due to disappointing performance in 1999 and 2000. As growth stock investors fled the stock, it became cheap enough to attract the attention of some value investors. As shown in the RDY chart in Figure 3.4, the stock had never been this cheap since 1962 when the data first became available.

At the time, JNJ was facing a number of internal and external challenges. The threat of political pressure and/or legislation to curb the industry's pricing was pressuring the stock prices of many firms in the pharmaceutical sector. Add to that several drugs facing patent expiration and the removal of Propulsid (heartburn medication) from the market due to rising fatalities, and it was easy to see why the stock price plunged so dramatically. Clearly, earnings growth momentum had stalled, and growth stock investors were tripping over each other to unload their holdings.

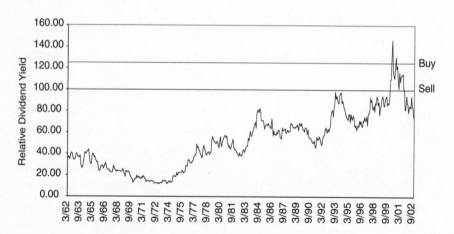

Figure 3.4 Johnson & Johnson (JNJ) Relative Dividend Yield
Source: Data from Compustat.

However, RDY focuses the value investor's attention on valuation. This was a company with a powerful consumer and pharmaceutical franchise. Through acquisitions, JNJ had one of the largest biotechnology franchises in the industry. Based on the historically high RDY the stock was trading at, the market was clearly not attributing value to many of JNJ's underlying, industry-leading businesses. When one class of investors sheds a holding, there can easily be a valuation mismatch for a moderately long period of time. If the underlying fundamentals are sound (see Chapter 5), this is usually a remarkably good time to begin accumulating the stock.

This was true in the case of JNJ. Value investors using the RDY discipline were able to capture the inefficiency in the stock price as growth investors fled the stock, and buyers were scarce.

It is important to note that, in certain situations, RDY does not work or no longer works. The primary example of when this comes into play is when RDY and Relative Price[2] are not correlated. A good illustration of this is the electric utilities industry. As shown in Figure 3.5, American Electric Power's

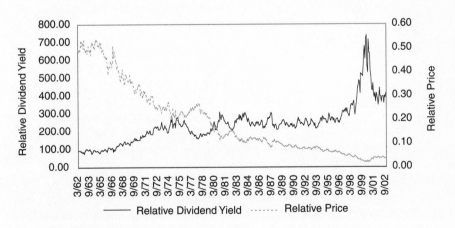

Figure 3.5 American Electric Power (AEP) Relative Dividend Yield and Relative Price
Source: Data from Compustat.

RDY and Relative Price disconnected (note the continual decline in Relative Price.) RDY charts for other utilities showed the same pattern, indicating that RDY is not an appropriate way to evaluate stocks in that sector. This situation can also occur on an individual stock basis, which is why the pattern of RDY to Relative Price must be checked whenever one evaluates a new stock with the RDY methodology.

The value of RDY as an investment tool is that it provides a rational, nonemotional basis for making sound investment decisions. RDY does not prevent emotionalism in investing, but it provides high-quality information and real notice of prevailing sentiment. When individuals are turning against a stock by selling it, the dividend yield will go up. It is that simple fact which makes RDY a reliable methodology for determining when a stock reaches a price range in which it might be bought, if the fundamentals are also there.

RDY works very well as an investment methodology. The results convinced us that we were on the right track with the new investment discipline. Ultimately, the economy would evolve, and this evolution would limit the universe of stocks for RDY investors, and consequently the ability of RDY alone to deliver returns that were consistent with the very best fund managers.

NOTES

1. *Relative Dividend Yield: Common Stock Investing for Income and Appreciation* (Wiley 1992) by Anthony Spare and Nancy Tengler provides a more detailed explanation of the development and implementation of RDY.

2. Relative Price is the price of the stock versus the price of the S&P 500. When first charting a stock, it is important to chart Relative Price over time to ensure that Relative Price is not showing a pattern of continual decline.

4

THE CHALLENGES OF
THE 1990s

"There was a time when a fool and his money were soon parted, but now it happens to everybody."

Adlai Stevenson

From the 1970s, when the team at Union Bank of California first began to experiment with Relative Dividend Yield (RDY), until the present time, RDY has consistently identified opportunities to acquire attractively priced stocks and sell stocks that have reached relatively high valuations. What has changed over time is the characteristics of the available pool of stocks. In the 1990s, investors placed less emphasis on dividends, and the number of stocks not paying a dividend increased from 10 percent of the S&P 500 in 1984 to 18 percent of the S&P 500 in June 2002. Moreover, the yield on the S&P 500 has declined to levels that have stabilized below 2 percent, despite the sustained pull back in the market over the last few years. In addition to an increase in the number of stocks not paying a dividend, there has been a rise in the number of stocks paying a modest dividend. In summary, over the last twenty years, the characteristics of the S&P 500 have become decidedly more "growthy." By the latter part of the 1990s, several generally non-dividend-paying sectors were becoming increasingly important in the economy. The rise of technology stocks, driven first by client-server computer technology and later by the Internet; the rise of health care stocks and biotechnology, in particular; and the shift in communications from a wired world run by regulated utilities to a wireless world all changed the face of the investment horizon.

This phenomenon changed the dynamics of the investor landscape and would later drive a dramatic shift in the composition of the S&P 500 Index (see Figure 1.2 on page 9) and the Dow Jones Industrial Average (DJIA). In computers, for example, IBM, which for years had been the dominant company in the field and a relatively high-yielding stock, was, perhaps, the premiere paradigm of an old-fashioned growth stock. By the early 1990s, it looked to be in terminal decline. Its stock price had fallen in value by more than half. Experts were trumpeting the end of the mainframe as PC manufacturers like Compaq and Dell were growing at a rapid clip. It would take the better part of a decade for IBM to transform itself back into a market leader, but in the process, the company slashed its dividend and laid off a large portion of its workforce. Meanwhile, companies like Intel and Microsoft paid little or no dividend, investing their excess cash to develop innovative products. Each grew to be market dominators in their own fields, with market capitalizations that would far exceed IBM's. These companies and other category leaders like them were beyond the reach of RDY.

In health care, the issues were much the same. Biotech companies such as Amgen and Genentech began to enter a new phase of drug discovery. No longer one-drug companies, biotech pipelines were burgeoning as big pharmaceutical companies were seeing the cost of drug development rising exponentially while productivity was declining. In the pharmaceutical sector, growth-oriented firms captured the attention of investors and the market. Dividend yield was not an important component of total return to these investors as cash was much better capitalized in the research and development budget than paid out in dividends. RDY investors were limited in their ability to play in this pond.

The picture was no different in telecommunications. In 1984, AT&T, the world's largest regulated utility, was broken up with the goal of stimulating more competition, and presumably lower prices and better telephone service. This resulted from a more than decade-long fight between AT&T and MCI, a small upstart company that had originally provided radio services to truckers. Almost immediately following deregulation, MCI became a formidable competitor to AT&T in long distance service, as did Sprint, a company spun off from GTE (an operator of small, local telephone companies around the United States). Meanwhile, other companies quickly attracted capital to compete with the regional Bell operating companies in offering local and regional service. Competition increased still further with the rise of cellular technology. Cellular was capital intensive and depended upon extremely rapid growth to attract capital. Needless to say, dividends were not a priority to these companies.

All three of these increasingly important sectors had one major trait in common: companies in these sectors believed they had to reinvest both in product development and in infrastructure to grow faster. These investments would translate into higher total return for their investors, a much more attractive alternative to paying out dividends as a way to generate returns for investors. This is typical of true growth companies and, at the time, the market agreed that growth was king. When the aggressive reinvestment/growth process works, as with a company such as Intel or Microsoft, it provides investors with strong incentives to purchase the stock for the increases in top-line revenue and bottom-line earnings growth. In the late 1990s, this happened when investors bid up the P/E ratio of the stocks to levels not seen since the Nifty Fifty bull market. However, earnings growth was robust and it seemed to investors (as it often does) that earnings would continue indefinitely on this double-digit growth trajectory.

In this environment, dividends were irrelevant. Attracting capital (which is, after all, the purpose of issuing stock) became more a function of persuading investors of a company's ability to produce exponential growth than a function of persuading them that the company could provide a superior return on invested capital (ROIC). If both were possible, so much the better, but for much of the decade of the 1990s, the emphasis was on growth for an America that was shaking off the final remnants of its old industrial culture.

Although the reference to the "old economy" versus the "new economy" has taken on a different meaning since the Internet/tech bubble burst, there has been an important secular change in the structure of the U.S. economy and the U.S. stock market. The U.S. economy has evolved from an industrial, manufacturing economy with heavy dependence on natural resources and labor to a service economy and now a "networked economy." Brian Wesbury writes about the "networked economy" in his book *The New Era of Wealth:*

> The networked economy is reducing the cost of information while increasing its value. As John Browning and Spencer Reiss in *Wired magazine* have pointed out, the very first fax machine ever built was worth absolutely nothing (even though it may have cost a bundle to build). The reason: There were no other machines to fax to, or to receive faxes from; however, the second fax machine was worth something and it made the first machine worth something as well. From that point on, every fax machine that is added to the worldwide network of fax machines not only increases the value of the very first fax machines, but it also increases the value of the entire network of fax machines.[1]

This phenomenon has been referred to by Kevin Kelly (author of *New Rules for the New Economy*[2]) as the "law of increasing returns." In the networked economy the value increases with the growth of the network. Every additional member exponentially impacts the productivity of the existing members of the network. It is not a zero-sum game. Growth is contagious and only serves to improve the productivity of the network participants—in this case, the U.S. economy.

Productivity has continued to enjoy strong growth, despite the recent economic slowdown that was catalyzed by the 2001 terrorist attacks on the World Trade Center and the Pentagon.

Consider the recent data for non-farm productivity:[3]

I September 2001 quarter: + 1.1 percent
I December 2001 quarter: + 5.5 percent
I March 2002 quarter: + 8.4 percent
I September 2002 quarter: + 4.0 percent (preliminary)

AN HISTORICAL VIEW OF U.S. PRODUCTIVITY

Although the Internet and technology stock values have declined precipitously, the *benefits* of the Internet are just beginning to take hold. The astute investor, the *value* investor, had to ferret through the "new economy"/"old economy" headlines and determine reality. Would business-to-consumer applications on the Internet replace traditional retailing, or was the Internet simply another form of distribution for retailers? Would AOL's or Amazon's market cap continue to outpace that of established, profitable corporations, or would market forces correct some of these outsized market caps back to levels supported by the underlying fundamentals? (See Figure 4.1.)

Wall Street has an unusual tendency to take recent events and extrapolate them out to infinity—as witnessed by the lofty valuations many of these stocks carried despite sketchy fundamentals. The valuation imbalance, which existed not just for months, but years, was enough to test even the most disciplined value investor.

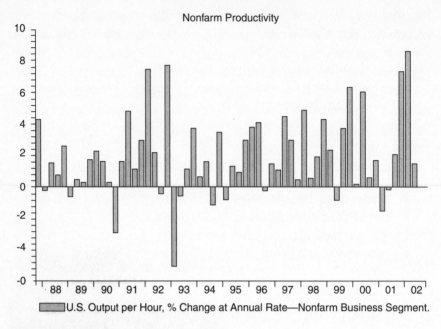

Figure 4.1   Non-Farm U.S. Productivity
Source: Data from Bureau of Labor Statistics.

The challenge for value-oriented investors in this economy and, in particular, managers who were dependent on yield or relative yield was to find a discipline that would identify the undervalued stocks in these sectors—a discipline that was tied back to company fundamentals and financial characteristics that could be measured and analyzed. The interest was not in the unproven, emerging companies, but rather in identifying the industry leaders in these "growthier" sectors of the market, so that, through careful analysis and rigorous valuation metrics, the "fallen angels"—the value stocks—could be identified.

In this new market environment, it was clear that RDY alone, limited as it was to dividend-paying stocks only, could not provide an entry point. We needed a valuation methodology that was as effective as RDY in consistently identifying opportune times to enter and exit a particular stock. The difficulty was identifying a meaningful valuation benchmark that could reliably provide good candidates across a more diversified universe of stocks. My long-time partner, Noel DeDora, and I began searching for a means to track periods of over- and undervaluation in companies paying low or no dividends. In starting this endeavor we focused our efforts on trying to find a stable indicator of value, similar to what we had achieved with the use of RDY.

The obvious place to start was with earnings. However, we immediately ran head-on into the earnings conundrum that had always reinforced the inherent value of RDY: Reported earnings do not always reflect a company's true earnings power. The superiority of RDY as a valuation benchmark was in the stability of the dividend. It didn't cycle with earnings. In fact, in the companies we owned, the dividend was set by management and the Board of Directors as a portion of *long-term, sustainable earnings power*. In short, the dividend normalized earnings growth over time. To make matters even more complex, the kinds of companies we were now considering typically had earnings that were cyclical or seasonal in nature.

There is nothing wrong with cyclical earnings. But, for a valuation benchmark to be effective, it must be consistent. By definition, cyclical earnings are not consistent. However, the concerns with earnings extended beyond the cyclicality that might be encountered. The reliability of earnings was also a problem. Under GAAP, managements are given discretion in how earnings are reported. Inventory accounting and depreciation schedules, for example, allow management considerable flexibility. In the 1990s, the increasing frequency of restructuring charges led analysts to focus more on operating earnings. Although there is no standardized definition of operating earnings, the objective was to identify the core sustainable earnings power of a company. However, if the definition of operating earnings was not standard, it would not meet the standard for consistency.[4,5] For those reasons, an earnings benchmark would not do, and the search for a stable, consistent valuation benchmark continued.

After again eliminating earnings as a potential benchmark, a number of other factors were considered until sales was settled on. Sales are not generally subjected to the vagaries of accounting methodologies. Sales are, well, sales! Top-line growth offered a good indicator of the status of the company's business and was not as vulnerable to manipulation as the earnings numbers.[6] The use of sales would come closest to offering the kind of stability and reliability we had experienced with dividends.

For perspective, Figures 4.2 through 4.4 show the relationship of sales versus earnings and illustrate the relative stability of sales when compared to the more volatile earnings data based on percentage change.

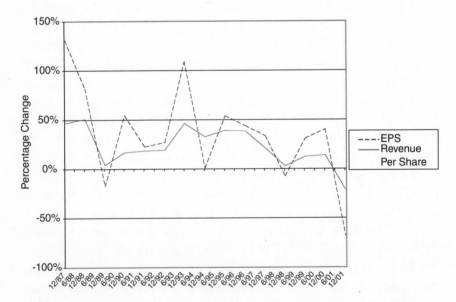

Figure 4.2 Intel Corp. (INTC) Percentage Change—Revenue Per Share versus Earnings Per Share
Source: Data from Bloomberg.

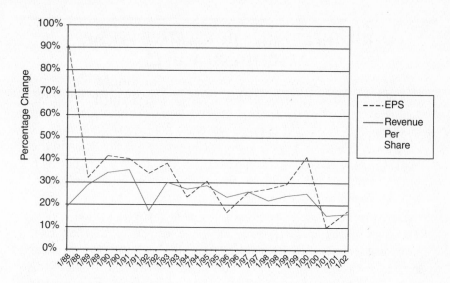

Figure 4.3 Home Depot (HD) Percentage Change—Revenue Per Share versus Earnings Per Share
Source: Data from Bloomberg.

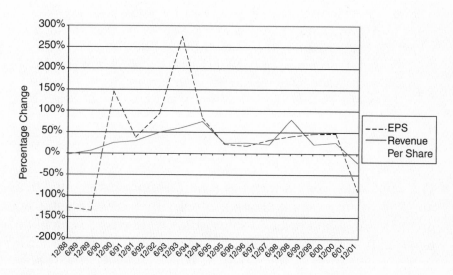

Figure 4.4 EMC (EMC) Percentage Change—Revenue Per Share versus Earnings Per Share
Source: Data from Bloomberg.

THE IMPORTANCE OF RELATIVE VERSUS ABSOLUTE MEASURES

One of the early lessons we learned as value investors was that value was relative, rather than absolute. The original Graham and Dodd methodology was based upon an absolute notion of value. A stock either was or was not priced below or above where it should be in the market on any given day, as represented by the relationship between price, earnings, and dividend yield. From the early days of using RDY we found the relative nature of the discipline to be one of its most useful features. Some stocks, like banks, always sold at a yield premium to the market. However, when compared to their own historical yield versus the market, there were definite periods when the stock was overvalued and undervalued. The *relative* nature of the discipline allowed us to identify cheap and dear stocks in any market environment and made it unnecessary for us to search for absolute yield hurdles (in effect, "junk stocks") as the market yield declined steadily in the 1990s. As value investors, we have viewed our charge as finding the most attractively valued stocks available for purchase in any given market environment. Relative value investing does not lead investors to the "lesser of two evils," but rather to stocks that are cheap based on their own historical valuation *and* relative to the market. Beginning with RDY and moving to RPSR, it is possible to apply the spirit of value investing to a much larger universe of stocks and identify value in *all* kinds of markets—our Relative Value Discipline.

The same sales versus earnings relationship was repeated in a number of large capitalization stocks that were paying no dividend. Absolute price-to-sales ratios were easy to calculate and told the investor how much he or she was paying for each unit of sales. It was shown that, as with dividends, it was possible to get a better and more consistent read on valuation by looking at sales from a relative perspective. A relative valuation methodology tells investors how attractive a particular stock is compared to other stocks and the market as a whole. Using a relative methodology provided an easier way to compare multiple companies within a given industry. The relative valuations assigned by the market demonstrated how investors valued one stock over another. This clearly was a pretty good indicator of where investors think a company's future prospects are headed. Committed to the results and information provided by a relative approach, we developed Relative Price-to-Sales Ratio (RPSR) as our valuation benchmark for non- or low-dividend-paying stocks.

RPSR compares a stock's historical price-to-sales ratio to the historical price-to-sales ratio of the S&P 500. When the stock's price-to-sales ratio is at the low end of its historical range versus the market, it is an attractive point at which to consider buying a stock. When the price-to-sales ratio is at the high end of its historical range, it has reached a valuation level that has historically represented a selling opportunity.

In looking at the RPSR history of numerous stocks, the relative price-to-sales ratio consistently provided important valuation information at turning points. RPSR, graphed over a reasonable period of time, identified periods of over- and undervaluation for a whole new universe of stocks.

CAN RPSR BE USED TO EVALUATE STOCKS OF ALL MARKET CAPS?

While the RPSR discussion has focused on large cap stock investing, RPSR can also be used to evaluate stocks ranging from small cap to large cap (as long as the companies have a meaningful sales history). It is interesting to note that RPSR was first considered in the context of small cap stocks. Noel DeDora and I had been asked to manage a portfolio of small cap value stocks, and obviously RDY would not work, so we began modeling RPSR with small cap stocks. The data was hard to find, making the use of RPSR cumbersome. As our investment universe for large cap portfolios began to narrow we then considered RPSR for larger cap stocks as well. By that time, the data was readily available and we could instantly graph the RPSR history of the stocks we were considering.

Before talking more about the "why" of RPSR, let's discuss the "what" and "how" of RPSR. The formula for calculating RPSR is:

$$\text{PSR*} = \frac{\text{Price of a Stock}}{\text{Sales per share}}$$

$$\text{RPSR} = \frac{\text{Stock's PSR}}{\text{S\&P 500 PSR}}$$

*Price-to-Sales Ratio

Figure 4.5 illustrates how RPSR is used to screen stocks (with primary applicability to stocks that pay little or no dividends). The sell range lies above the higher of the two lines, and the buy range lies below the lower of the two lines. In the case of RPSR analysis, the buy and sell levels are set at

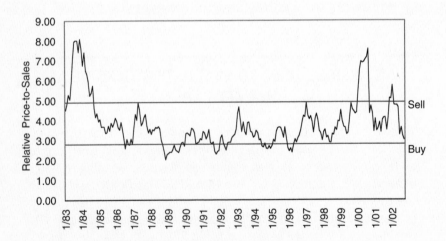

Figure 4.5 Company ABC Relative Price-to-Sales
Source: Data from Compustat.

one standard deviation below and above the stock's average RPSR for the period 12/31/92 to the most recent month (charts show history back to 1984 for perspective.) Monthly data points are used to calculate this average. The anchor date was set at 12/31/92 for two reasons:

1. If the data was not anchored on at least one end, there would be, in some instances, too much volatility in the ranges. This was caused by the impact of changing both the beginning and ending data points during periods of high volatility in sales, which resulted in range changes of excessive magnitudes. Anchoring the beginning point reduces this effect to manageable levels.

2. Our proprietary research showed that the quality and reliability of the data starting in late 1992 was superior to that previously available and not subject to survivorship bias.[7]

It is important to note that the charts in this book reflect month-end data. It is not unusual for a company to come into a buy or sell range on an intra-month basis, which may not be reflected in the charts as shown. The RDY and RPSR examples detailed later in the book will have that fact pointed out.

In looking at adopting sales as a valuation indicator, we immediately began comparing it to the information received through the dividend. One of the most critical differences was that sales, although a somewhat stable indicator, did not provide the company insight that the dividend offered due to the deliberate nature with which corporate boards set their dividends—we would have to account for this in our fundamental research process (discussed in Chapter 5).

To test the RPSR methodology, two things were considered:

1. For companies amenable to both RDY and RPSR analysis, would RPSR work synchronously with RDY, or would they contradict each other?

2. In what circumstances would RPSR *not* work?

The first test of the RPSR hypothesis as a good valuation benchmark was whether RPSR would bring the same conclusions as RDY for stocks on which both methodologies could be applied. We found, in fact, that the buy/sell signals of the two valuation approaches were very closely correlated, as illustrated in Figures 4.6, 4.7, and 4.8. (It is important to note that although RDY and RPSR appear to be inversely correlated, they are actually positively correlated and only appear inversely correlated because the buy and sell lines are reversed; in other words, RDY signals a buy on the higher of the two lines, while RPSR signals a buy on the lower of the two lines.) This correlation was a powerful indicator found repeatedly in the examined companies. RPSR identified similar valuation opportunities obtained by using RDY. It is important to note here that while

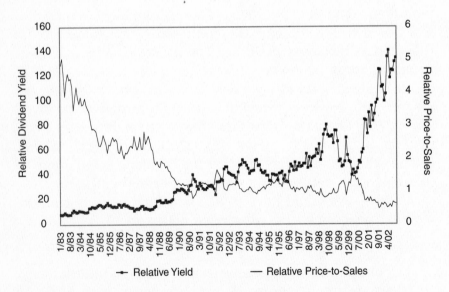

Figure 4.6 Hewlett Packard (HPQ) Relative Dividend Yield and Relative Price-to-Sales Ratio
Source: Data from Compustat.

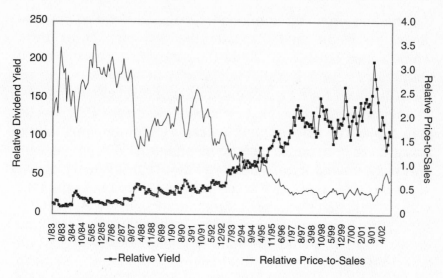

Figure 4.7 Limited Brands (LTD) Relative Dividend Yield and Relative Price-to-Sales Ratio
Source: Data from Compustat.

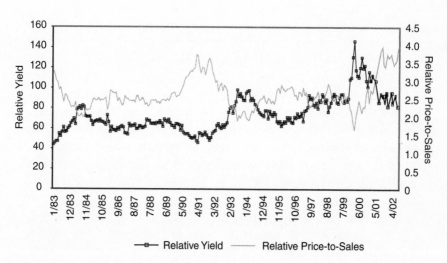

Figure 4.8 Johnson & Johnson (JNJ) Relative Dividend Yield versus Relative Price-to-Sales Ratio
Source: Data from Compustat.

this finding provided confidence in the investment methodology, we would find out later that in some cases RPSR
would signal buys too early in the case of stocks that would
ultimately become buyable under RDY at much lower prices
(See Chapter 7 for a further discussion of this phenomenon).

Inevitably, there would be companies where RPSR was not
applicable. The primary and logical area of non-applicability
was growth companies with no meaningful sales or, more importantly, no history of sales. We knew that these firms were
of no interest to us—we were only interested in companies
with established businesses. Most importantly, we knew that
RPSR, like RDY, was simply an indication of value—not quality. In order to avoid "terminally cheap" stocks we would
have to conduct rigorous fundamental work (see Chapter 5).
At this point we decided to begin testing RPSR in actual practice. As with RDY, we would couple the RPSR methodology
with our approach to fundamental analysis.

THE MECHANICS OF RPSR

In using RPSR, you initially need to determine the universe of
stocks that will potentially be candidates for RPSR analysis.
Compustat (an institutional research provider), for example, may be
used to narrow the universe to companies with market capitalizations of over $3 billion, if your charge is to fish in the large cap
pool of stocks. However, RPSR can be used in the mid- and small
cap arenas as well.

The next step is to construct the RPSR charts for each company.
(This information is generally only available to institutional
investors through services such as Compustat.) We update our charts
once a month using month-end information. A spreadsheet is constructed for each stock. Next you see a sample of a worksheet section that we use in our analysis:

Date	Relative Price-to-Sales	Relative Price	Buy	Sell	Average	Std
1/83	3.168897084	0.038497939	2.2183285	3.2241004	2.721214	0.5029
2/83	3.199694831	0.038835608	2.2183285	3.2241004		
3/83	3.241308566	0.040451754	2.2183285	3.2241004		
4/83	2.816401252	0.035161477	2.2183285	3.2241004		
5/83	2.65249409	0.033099329	2.2183285	3.2241004		
6/83	2.839823007	0.034854414	2.2183285	3.2241004		
7/83	2.872931639	0.035275437	2.2183285	3.2241004		
8/83	2.811696266	0.034500457	2.2183285	3.2241004		
9/83	3.087106788	0.036411605	2.2183285	3.2241004		
10/83	3.448484216	0.040698566	2.2183285	3.2241004		
11/83	3.37792212	0.039813703	2.2183285	3.2241004		

To calculate Relative Price-to-Sales you need to divide the Price-to-Sales of the Stock by the Price-to-Sales of the S&P 500. (See page 44 for the RPSR formula.)

Next, you need to do the calculations to set the buy/sell lines. To do this, first find the mean RPSR for each month for the period 12/31/92 to the current month. Then calculate the standard deviation of the RPSRs over that period of time. Set the buy line at one standard deviation under the mean RPSR for that period. Set the sell line at one standard deviation above the mean RPSR for that period. On a monthly basis you should update the charts and the buy/sell lines to include the most recent month's data.

To maintain the charts, once you have them in place, generally review them on a monthly basis. If particular issues are more active, you can look at the charts on a daily basis.

NOTES

1. Brian Wesbury, *The New Era of Wealth: How Investors Can Profit From the Five Economic Trends Shaping the Future* (McGraw-Hill, 1999).
2. Kevin Kelly, *New Rules for the New Economy: 10 Radical Strategies for a Connected World* (Penguin USA, 1999).

3. Non-farm productivity growth is typically measured by the quarter-to-quarter change in output per hour of all persons in the business sector (seasonally adjusted and measured by the Bureau of Labor Statistics).

4. Enron and WorldCom both provide extreme examples of the lack of a standard definition of operating earnings and criminal abuse of the system. In 2001, Enron was forced to restate earnings back to 1997 based on inappropriate accounting of loans. In 2002, with the discovery of WorldCom's nearly $4 billion in inappropriately accounted for expenditures, the company was pushed into bankruptcy.

5. As a further indication of the overall problems with earnings figures, the June 22, 2002, issue of the *Economist* stated "almost 1,000 American companies have now restated their earnings since 1997, admitting in effect that they had previously published wrong or misleading numbers."

6. Sales figures can be subject to some manipulation. For example, we recently saw that situation related to capacity swaps in the telecom industry and round trip contracts in the major power brokerage companies. Our assessment is that these situations are rare and therefore do not pose a significant threat to our investment discipline.

7. Survivorship bias refers to the fact that most data providers only provide access to data on the current holdings in the S&P 500. Therefore, when using historical data, the further you go back, the more the data is skewed due to the changing nature of the indices. Of the 500 stocks in the Index today, dozens were not in the Index ten years ago.

5

THE TWELVE FUNDAMENTAL FACTORS OF RDY AND RPSR RESEARCH

"Even if you're on the right track, you'll get run over if you just sit there."

Will Rogers

While RDY and RPSR are powerful indicators of periods of over- and undervaluation, they comprise only the first step in our valuation process, since stocks are sometimes cheap for good reason. We want to avoid those stocks—the stocks we like to call "terminally cheap." We need to ensure that we are not falling into the value manager trap—buying and holding and watching these stocks as they become even cheaper. To avoid this, stocks that pass the RDY or RPSR screens are subjected to rigorous qualitative and quantitative analysis. In order for a stock to reach the stage where we would consider investing in it, it must pass through a twelve-factor screening process, with positive results on at least two of the three qualitative factors, and five of the nine quantitative factors.

Noel DeDora and I began developing this approach, which we now call the *Twelve Fundamental Factors*, in the early 1990s. We had observed that while our valuation screens were effective, they could not protect us from the purchase of a company whose stock price reflected underlying weak fundamentals. At the very least, we risked owning stocks that would languish as the market rose or, worse, decline further. We determined that in our fundamental analysis process we needed the same rigorous discipline our valuation work produced. Working with our team of analysts, we identified twelve factors that were important measures of a company's underlying health. We believed consistent adherence to this research discipline would reduce the possibility of holding cheap stocks that would remain cheap for good fundamental reasons.

Over time, we have found that the core of the Twelve Fundamental Factors has remained consistent, but we have made minor changes in the criteria to address the evolving market and the dynamic universe of stocks we draw from. The factors were designed to capture the essence of the important issues facing value investors. In summary form, here is the checklist that is currently used:

TWELVE FUNDAMENTAL FACTORS CHECKLIST

Qualitative (2 of 3)	Y	N	Quantitative (5 of 9)	Y	N
Buggy Whip			Sales/Revenue Growth		
Franchise or Niche Value			Operating Margins		
Top Management and Board of Directors			Relative P/E		
			Positive Free Cash Flow		
			Dividend Coverage and Growth		
			Asset Turnover		
			Investment in Business/ROIC		
			Equity Leverage		
			Financial Risk		

The following pages describe this analytical process. As you read the chapter, it may also be useful to reference Appendix B, C and D, which include samples of the Twelve Fundamental Factors put into practice.

QUALITATIVE APPRAISAL

The Buggy Whip Factor

The "Buggy Whip" factor is meant to address product and/or service obsolescence. Throughout history, stocks often become cheap when there is some question about a product's long- or short-term viability. Therefore, it's best to examine a company's products and technology from several perspectives, such as product acceptance in the marketplace and the percentage of revenue a company derives from new and existing products. These are the more straightforward quantitative approaches to the problem.

More importantly, one should consider the qualitative factors surrounding the company. Take JC Penney (JCP), a company we gave a failing grade in 1998 on the Buggy Whip factor. The reason for the fail was based on our perceptions of the retail market at that time and JCP's position in the full-service department store segment. The retail market had become bifurcated into two distinct segments: upscale/specialty and deep discount. JCP was neither. The best chance it had was on the discount end of the market where Sears offered lower price points and held the dominant share. Target and Wal-Mart were delivering fashion on the cheap and steadily encroaching on JCP's market share. This led us to believe that JCP's store model was becoming a legacy of the past and we therefore failed it on the buggy whip factor. With new management, JCP ultimately right-sized the company, but to date the stock price has not come close to reaching the price levels the stock was sold at following our disciplined look at the twelve factors.

As each company is evaluated, consider the question, "Are the company's products viable today and into the foreseeable future?"

Franchise or Niche Value

When buying value stocks—that is, stocks that are undervalued due to market underperformance—look for stocks that have a strong product franchise. Market leaders have pricing power and purchasing power

$$\text{Pricing power} + \text{Purchasing power} = \text{Strong margins and Flexibility}$$

With good management (the next factor) this combination should generate superior earnings growth over time. A stock may be undervalued due to a problem with its products or its profitability, but at the end of the day the chances are much better that the company will be able to fix the problem if it is dealing from a position of strength. This factor emphasizes the importance of leadership and the resulting "mind share" accorded to leaders in the marketplace. Industry dominance does not ensure a company won't stumble, but it does increase the odds that a company can right itself.

Nike (NKE), for example, is the franchise leader in shoes, producing a franchise that is recognized worldwide. NKE started to build its brand recognition with famed American distance runner Steve Prefontaine and the running shoe. However, Michael Jordan's affiliation with NKE in 1985 revolutionized industry marketing practices. NKE's development of Brand Jordan and the overflow of that brand into other sports categories is responsible for a significant portion of the athletic footwear sales growth throughout the decade. Jordan and Brand Jordan really put the NKE swoosh on the map. Moreover, rather than resting on its laurels with Jordan, NKE attached other unique personalities to the swoosh. Nike Town stores and Tiger Woods have helped continue the strong franchise value of NKE in the 1990s. The power of that brand's dominance and the NKE swoosh drives fashion cycles. NKE is well positioned to respond or adapt to changes as the market leader. The same thing can be said for Gillette in personal care products. Gillette "owns" shaving in a way that no other company can.

Owning a brand can be a critical component of franchise value, particularly in the consumer nondurable sector. Strong evidence of this fact can be found in a 1994 study done by London-based Interbrand Corp. in which the strongest brands in England in 1933 were shown to still be the market leaders in 1994, more than sixty years later. Hoover was still number one in vacuum cleaners; in fact, Britons don't vacuum their carpets and floors, they "hoover" them. Colgate was still number one in toothpaste, Gillette was still number one in razors, and Cadbury's was still number one in chocolates. If you look at the U.S. market, this same branding trend holds true. Few competitors have ever been able to displace a company that gains mindshare through brand dominance.

Questions to consider in looking at franchise or niche value include:

1. **Is the company profitably maintaining/gaining market share?** Finding growing companies is critical to any investment strategy. It is best to avoid firms that are struggling to maintain position. Chrysler is a good example. The company, although it had a strong brand, was plagued by poor product quality and declining perception in the market. Additionally, it did not hold a leadership position as the number three player in auto sales in the United States. Without a dominant market share and with a product plagued by quality concerns, Chrysler did not meet the criteria of this factor. Once it's established that a company has a strong product offering, the question is whether that product line is being effectively used to spur profitable growth.

2. **Can the company leverage its franchise to enter new markets profitably over time?** As markets become saturated and mature, a company has to be able to extend its franchise in order to continue to grow. In the 1990s, companies began to successfully portray

their brands as "lifestyle" choices. Nike was able to jump from shoes into athletic wear with strong approval from consumers. IBM, which made desktop computers, became a major supplier of Internet services, using the computer as the starting point of entry into the World Wide Web. Mercedes-Benz became a dominant player in the burgeoning sport utility vehicle market by building a rugged, stylish SUV that was priced reasonably, but had all the amenities and cachet of a Mercedes. When a company can leverage its brand into new areas that make sense given its business model, and can therefore extend the franchise, the company has a better chance of holding its dominance within its respective industry.

3. **Has franchise value (the earnings driver of the company) increased over time?** This is really a combination of the first and second questions. It is not enough to maintain or gain market share, and it is not enough to enter new markets. A company has to be recognized for its efforts in the marketplace, and be rewarded for it by investors. The critical factors for companies successfully passing this test are their ability to deliver quality offerings and, on an ongoing basis, their ability to develop new products and get them to market in a cost effective/profitable manner. Intel is a good example of a company that has a strong history of sustained increases in franchise value. Intel's earnings have grown from just over $1 billion in 1992 to $10.5 billion in 2000, (well ahead of the average company in the S&P 500) while at the same time it has built a reputation based on continuous innovation and delivery of a high-quality product. Pricing power goes to the market leaders; for a company like Intel, this means it can set a competitive market price and maintain profit margins while investing in future product innovations to maintain its dominant position.

Top Management and Board of Directors

Buyers of value stocks must view themselves as investors—not traders. They are not merely trading paper, they are buying the company. That means they are buying the product, the margins, the balance sheet—and most importantly—the management team.

This is by far the most important and the most difficult factor to assess, and it can be even more difficult in today's environment where executives are much more mobile. Time and observation has taught investors to be somewhat skeptical of CEOs brought in from outside the corporation. Certainly they *can* succeed, but large cap companies frequently have such an ingrained culture that a CEO brought in from the outside can have a difficult time getting traction. This observation is reinforced by an argument that Jim Collins makes in his book *Good to Great*: "larger-than-life, celebrity leaders who ride in from the outside are negatively correlated with taking a company from good to great."[1]

Because management is a critical factor in the success or failure of a company, it's best to take a closer than average look at the management of companies that one is considering for investment. Most fund managers pay at least some lip service to assessing a company's Board and executives. Since as value investors, we prefer to hold onto a stock for some time, sound, stable, long-term management is an absolute requirement.

Questions to consider when examining a company from a management perspective include:

1. **What is the strength of a company's management depth and culture?** Does the company have a culture of accountability? Is there accountability for overall revenue and expenses from the CEO's office all the way down the line to low-level managers? A good example of this type of company is Wells Fargo, which focused its efforts in the 1970s on hiring the right people to ensure that a strong management team would be in place to

face the challenges in the industry. At the same time, the company created a culture of accountability.

Related to accountability, companies that create an environment of vested interest in the success of the company are desirable. Certain other factors, such as excessive turnover and/or a lack of a succession plan, should create cause for concern.

2. **Is the management compensation plan tied to increasing shareholder value?** This is one of the trickiest issues to evaluate, since so many companies now give their executives stock options in place of, or in addition to, cash bonuses. At the time of this writing, options don't show up as a balance sheet expense, so companies are quite willing to be liberal with them. Compensation programs are best evaluated through a detailed review of the proxy statement (in the past I have been amazed by how many Wall Street analysts overlook or only pay lip service to this valuable document). In reading the proxy statements, look for compensation plans that reward competence. If the CEO gets a big raise while earnings per share, market share, and so on are declining, it should be seen as a red flag. In addition, investors should look for compensation plans that are tied concretely to increasing shareholder value. Overall they should focus on firms that incent their executives over the long, rather than short, term and who reward quality growth and performance versus a peer group. These compensation plans can take the form of salaries, cash bonuses, options, and so on. Despite recent outcries over the accounting of stock options and stock ownership, we believe aligning shareholder and management interest is critical over the long term.

3. **Is the Board of Directors independent and relevant?** Every time there is a business scandal, the first question that everyone asks is, "Where was the Board in all

of this?" Investigate whether there is real involvement by the Board, or if the Board is simply cosmetic window-dressing. Specifically, investors should focus on the following:

A. The Size of the Board: A manageable Board with a size of up to twelve members is preferable.

B. Insiders versus Independents: A strong Board made up of a majority of outsiders with only one or two insiders is preferred.

C. Quality and Breadth of the Board: Ideal Board members actually add real value to the management oversight of a company. Their own experience and management depth can add strength in the areas key to corporate health: audit, finance, manufacturing, or marketing.

WHAT IS A PROBLEMATIC BOARD?

Heinz is a good example of a company that received a failing grade because of the Board. Here is what I wrote in 1998 in my column for the Strategy Lab of Microsoft Investor:

> The company has a 19-member board, which is high by our standards . . . we look for a more manageable board of around 12 members. But more important is that 10 (yes, 10!) of those members are insiders; we would prefer to see one or two. A number of the directors are well past 70, the mandatory retirement age at most publicly traded companies. That's OK with us, but we will express some surprise at the 85-year-old insider on the board; he must be a remarkable individual indeed! And the number of my countrymen from the old sod is worth noting.

> Now don't get me wrong. I would give my left brain to be invited to a party with these folks. O'Reilly is as charming and witty as the grass is green. And who could forget that jolly fellow, Tom

Foley, from his Speaker of the House days? Nicholas Brady from the Bush Administration? Ah yes, a fine bunch 'tis too. The party would be grand and would go on for hours with champagne and ketchup flowing while the partygoers regaled with hilarious story after hilarious story ... each person wishing they, too, could be Irish, with that incredible talent for happiness.

But would I start a business with these folks? Do they comprise the most relevant board for this branded-goods company? After all, they have no practical business experience by and large. Thankfully, they are overseeing a very strong management team that is highly incented to return to shareholders an above-market and peer-group return.[2]

April, 1998

THE TWELVE FUNDAMENTAL FACTORS ARE NOT FAIL-SAFE

Nothing is fail-safe. Despite great valuation tools and a disciplined approach to research, I have made a few investments I wish I hadn't. One worth noting was the purchase of *Reader's Digest* in the fall of 1995 when the stock was trading in the low $40s. The company passed the Twelve Fundamental Factors and was cheap according to RDY, but the fundamentals kept deteriorating. We examined the twelve factors again and failed the company in February 1997. We sold our position in the mid $30s and watched the stock plummet to below $20 by August 1998. While our absolute loss was not great, the opportunity cost was horrendous given the market's performance during the same period. Our mistake was giving a new management team too much credit, not focusing enough on the company's short life as a public company, and underestimating the impact of outside investors owning a class of "non-voting" shares in the company.

QUANTITATIVE APPRAISAL

The guidelines for reviewing each of the quantitative factors include:

- a brief discussion of the reason for including the factor,
- specific measures that should be applied in evaluating the factor, and
- suggested benchmarks for determining whether the company passes or fails on the factor.

When pertinent to the analysis of a potential investment, the inclusion of additional quantitative measures is strongly encouraged. The guidelines are intended to provide analytical relevance, a disciplined but flexible framework, and, in most cases, a comprehensive structure for evaluating investments across industries.

Sales/Revenue Growth

Sales growth is the cornerstone of the foundation for the overall investment case. At the most fundamental level, revenues measure the economic acceptance of the company's products and/or services and the competitiveness of the offerings relative to its peers. It is easy to identify and quantify. In evaluating sales/revenue growth, consider it as a measure that seeks to establish stable-to-improving growth trends that enhance the company's competitive position.

Components to consider in looking at sales/revenue growth include:

1. **Historical growth rates**. A company that learns how to generate consistent year-over-year growth is a winner in anyone's eyes. Stable sales growth provides powerful insight into data regarding the acceptance and growth of a company's products.

2. **Industry growth rate, influences, and trends**. The real measure of a company's revenue growth is its ability to continue growing even as a market begins to mature, when pricing, promotion, and positioning come into greater and greater play than product quality alone. Investors should not only examine absolute year-over-year growth, but also comparative growth within industry and product groups.

3. **Estimated long-term company growth rates and catalysts**. This is a somewhat qualitative call within a quantitative context. When we see a company growing strongly, the natural inclination is to ask, "How long can they keep it up?" and "What are the factors that could cause their growth to slow?" Some of those factors were alluded to earlier, such as management strength and depth, technological superiority, market dominance, product cycles, and obsolescence. In addition, it's also important to review internal company factors, such as the cost of sales, and the larger selling, general, & administrative (SG&A) figure. A company will often use accounting devices to lower its cost of sales, but will shift some of those costs over into the larger category of sales, general, and administrative. A rising SG&A or a rising cost of sales is an indication that the company is having to spend more to get each "next" dollar of sales. While the sales curve may continue to rise, the company and investors are eventually going to have to pay for it in some way.

4. **Declining, stable, or improving competitive position**. As noted in an earlier chapter, sales/revenue growth is a critical factor in this analysis. Companies are expected to use all means available to generate long-term sales growth, and their results are based upon where they are in the marketplace. It's important for investors to know that a company is doing the things it needs to in order to improve its competitive position, such as

making alliances with channel partners, improving the product range, strengthening the brand/franchise, and so on. When measuring competitive positioning, look at a company's market share data and sales growth in comparison to its competitors. It is also important to qualitatively evaluate how fast the company is innovating and adding new products, as well as if the company is entering new markets.

THE TWELVE FUNDAMENTAL FACTORS IN AN ERA OF ENRONS, WORLDCOMS, ADELPHIAS, AND SO ON

The best test of an investing strategy is how well it does when the market is not doing what it is expected to do. Since 1999, when drug distributor McKesson Corp. was rocked by an accounting scandal and was forced to restate its earnings, the anomaly has become the norm. In 2002, the stock market, already in a tailspin because of the implosion of Internet stocks, has been forced to take on almost daily doses of horrible news. One giant company after another, from Enron in September 2001, through Xerox, WorldCom, and Adelphia Communications, has been rocked by accounting scandals. Others, such as AOL Time Warner, have had to write down billions of dollars of shareholder value, and still others, such as conglomerate Tyco International Ltd., have watched their CEOs resign in disgrace for matters not related to company business. Each event has been followed by a sharp decline in share prices.

Fortunately for us, we managed to escape most of the damage. Our use of the Twelve Fundamental Factors pointed out a sufficient number of caveats early enough that we were able to shy away from most of the stocks that turned out to be problems. For example, when Tyco International reached our buy range, we didn't buy it, because of our growing fear that the company's debt could become unmanageable. We had no way of knowing that CEO Dennis Kozlowski would be indicted by the State of New York for sales tax fraud, but our fundamental analysis told us that in an economic downturn, the company would be hard-pressed to continue its growth strategy.

Calpine also came into our buy range, but after doing a quick analysis based on the Twelve Fundamental Factors, we were unable to understand the sustainability of its funding strategy and therefore decided to pass on the stock. Enron came into our buy range right after CEO Jeffrey Skilling unexpectedly resigned. While he was telling the press that he was leaving for personal reasons, several components of our Twelve Fundamental Factors approach told us that there were risks to the company.

These examples reinforce our commitment to always stick to our discipline. There are enough good companies that pass the Twelve Fundamental Factors and still generate disappointing returns. It's unnecessary to take risks with companies that do not meet your standards, no matter how attractive their valuations may seem at the time.

Operating Margins

Operating margins are a simple but fairly accurate measure of profitability. Stabilizing and/or improving margins, particularly for value stocks, portend well for upward valuation adjustments as the firm's competitive position is seen to stabilize and hopefully strengthen over time. For value managers who are typically accumulating stocks in periods of depressed margins, stabilization is an important sign that fundamentals are improving.

In evaluating operating margins, consider the following issues:

1. **Trend analysis of a firm's operating margins**. This analysis is very straightforward. Is the trend line rising or falling, and by how much? More important, is there a trend line? A company whose operating margins are erratic from year-to-year is one that is struggling to maintain its competitive position.

2. **A firm's operating margins relative to industry margins**. Just as with sales growth, comparing a company to its competitors suggests a lot. Investors should look for the best companies within any given industry

sector, because stock value is likeliest to rebound among the companies that have the best operating conditions—good operating margins give the management flexibility to use pricing to gain market share in difficult periods.

3. **A firm's operating margins, assuming a normal operating environment**. Sometimes the operating margins of either a firm or its industry sector will decline from a long-term trend line. If this is the case, look at the current operating margins and business environment to assess whether the company's operation is temporarily being impacted, or if the industry is in a secular decline. It is not unusual for us to buy a stock that is experiencing a temporary decline in operating margins.

4. **The level of revenue and assets necessary to sustain operating margins**. These are the ratios of sales-to-margin and assets-to-margin. A firm may be maintaining its operating margins, or even improving them, and still be in declining health if it takes an increasing amount of revenue to produce each incremental gain in margin. The same thing is true for assets. A company may be spending more and more on its next generation of plant and equipment for smaller and smaller incremental gains in operating margin, as the company's leverage begins to disappear in the face of market saturation, and increased competition.

CASE STUDY: 1997 FAILURE OF *READER'S DIGEST* ON OPERATING MARGINS

As an example of a failure on operating margins, here is an excerpt from a 1997 Twelve Fundamental Factors analysis on *Reader's Digest* (RDA):

On an absolute basis, RDA operating margins compare favorably to its peer group. Our peer group consisted of the following: Houghton Mifflin (HTN—educational publisher); K-III (KCC—largest direct marketer of children's books and publisher of over 40 trade magazines and 60 directories); McGraw-Hill (MHP—publishes consumer, trade and educational magazines); Meredith (MDP— publishes magazines targeted towards consumers in the home and family market); and Scholastic (SCHL—markets children's educational magazines and software via direct mail and developed the first animated science series on PBS).

From 1990 to 1996, RDA has consistently ranked second behind MHP. Five year average operating margins for RDA and MHP are 14.6% and 16.7%, respectively. CAGR for the same period has been −2.2% and −3.5%, respectively. The decline in MHP's operating margins can be attributed, somewhat, to the exchange of Shephard's for the Times Mirror Higher Education Group in October 1996. From 1995 to 1996, RDA's operating margins declined 146 basis points, from 14.6% to 13.0%. Management attributes this decline in performance to a flawed strategy of excess promotions (particularly in Europe); rising paper and postage prices; and limited channels of distribution, which inhibited the penetration rate of the company's 100 million customer database. Most of the competitors in the above listed peer group have communicated to us that they do anticipate "modest paper price increases" during the second half of 1997 and RDA is nearly complete with the restructuring of its European operations and cost improvement program. Going forward, this should provide some restoration of modest margin expansion. What we are seeking, however, is an acceleration of top-line growth, which RDA has consistently failed to provide.

For these reasons, we failed RDA on operating margins.
February, 1997

Relative P/E

The price-earnings ratio is the most frequently used and misused valuation ratio. Prudent valuation of a company's earnings potential includes market and peer group comparisons, factoring in past cycle valuations and growth rate assumptions.

In evaluating the price-earnings ratio, consider the following issues:

1. **Trailing, current, and forward P/E relative to the market and the peer group**. Wall Street has long had varying opinions about the value of earnings from company to company, and industry to industry. The value of earnings in an industry such as automobiles, which is capital intensive, versus the value of earnings in an innovative technology company with low to no levels of debt are different, and they should be. Therefore, when looking at earnings, it is important for investors to differentiate between individual company and industry dynamics.

2. **Trough earnings and peak earnings multiple for the company**. Many companies have earnings ranges that rise and fall with various factors, such as economic or industry cycles. The relative P/E of the company is of primary interest. Investors should look at historical P/Es over a long period and compare them to the market and the company's own history to identify peaks, troughs, and relative valuation ranges.

3. **Projected earnings in a "normal" operating environment**. This criterion relates to the previous one. Most companies examined are in a state of depressed earnings due to various factors including economic downturns. At these times it is important to look at what the earnings multiple would be in "normal" times, in order to gauge what the company might be worth under better business conditions (based on its own valuation history and industry benchmarks). This figure can then be compared to the current valuation to determine the relative attractiveness of the valuation.

4. **Improving or deteriorating normalized earnings relative to the last cycle**. This is an extension of the point previously made. Once investors come up with

normalized earnings, they can plot normalized earnings over time as a set of moving averages, and then calculate the percentage increase or decrease from normalized earnings. This reveals the company's long-term ability to generate earnings in good times or bad, which provides some clues about its future value. Investors should look for companies that have a consistent ability to improve their earnings at a faster rate than the industry as a whole in good times, and that do not deteriorate as rapidly as the industry as a whole in bad times. (This is often a function of leadership as discussed in the qualitative factor discussion of "Franchise or Niche Value.") Investors will pay more for the next dollar of earnings than the last, if they believe that a company can sustain its growth better than the competition.

5. **Projected EPS growth rate relative to the industry growth rate**. Investors should examine the current history of a company and the industry within which it operates and ask the question: "How much of the industry's growth will eventually show up on Company A's bottom line, compared to Company B's?" They then can look at the companies within the industry group and, on the basis of relative past performance and their knowledge of the company, make a judgment about whether earnings will increase, decrease, or remain flat.

Positive Free Cash Flow

The greater the cash flow, the greater the opportunity for management to increase shareholder value by either redeploying the proceeds into strategic growth areas or by simply returning the cash to shareholders via share repurchases or dividends. Improving working capital turnover and operating cash flow yield both signal financial flexibility.

Issues to examine regarding positive free cash flow include:

1. **The free cash flow trend**. Cash is almost always king in the market. The more cash a company has, the more it can do to improve its competitive position. Investors should look at cash flow on a five-year basis, and look for companies that are increasing their ability to generate cash flow year-over-year with cash flow defined as Operating net + DD&A – Capital spending – Common dividends.

2. **Trend in operating cash flow per share relative to EPS**. In the best companies, cash flow will rise at least as fast as earnings per share. Investors can calculate the percentage rise year-over-year for both and compare them. Again, the faster that cash flow rises, the more money that is available both for expansion and raising the dividend.

3. **Working capital turnover trend analysis relative to historic trends and the industry**. Working capital turnover is an indication of a company's operating efficiency and ability to internally fund new growth initiatives. Investors should compare a company's working capital turnover rate both with the company's own long-term averages, and with the industry's long-term average. The best companies will usually be turning capital over at a faster rate.

4. **Historic and projected ability of the company to fund its growth internally**. This is a very important factor. One of the reasons investors are so interested in cash flow is that it has a direct impact on the amount of capital a company might need to borrow in order to expand or maintain its business in a poor economic or interest rate climate. If a company has strong free cash flow and has built up reasonable cash reserves, consistent with its business needs, it can continue to do business during adverse conditions without borrowing, or it can expand in good times without taking on debt.

CASE STUDY: EASTMAN KODAK (EK)—FAIL POSITIVE FREE CASH FLOW

As an example of a failure in Positive Free Cash Flow, here is an excerpt from a 1998 Twelve Fundamental Factors analysis on Eastman Kodak (EK):

> In 1996, EK's free cash flow was marginally positive at $0.10 per share. In 1997, a combination of pricing competition from Fuji, a strong dollar, a lower level of depreciation, higher capital spending and a higher per share dividend rate resulted in negative free cash flow of $0.50 per share. Technically, the company meets our criterion of positive free cash flow (Operating Net + DD&A – Capital Spending – Common Dividends) in one of the last two years. However, EK's –0.8% free cash flow yield compares unfavorably with its peer group. Free cash flow yield for the group ranges from –0.8% to 4.0% with a 2.0% median. We are taking a cautious stance by failing the company on this factor.

February 1998

Dividend Coverage and Growth

In companies that pay dividends, there is often a "dividend-paying culture" that influences dividend policy. In fact, one of the most significant insights investors discern from RDY is based on dividend actions by the Board; investors can observe what management expects in terms of future long-term earnings growth. Bear in mind that many mature dividend-paying companies set the dividend level as a ratio/percentage of long-term sustainable earnings power. By analyzing the dividend history of a company, it is possible to gain an understanding of the firm's current and projected earnings growth rates.

Issues to examine regarding dividend coverage and growth include:

1. **The current payout ratio**. The payout ratio should reflect a reasonable ratio to earnings that is sustainable and in line with the industry. There are occasions where an entire industry's fundamentals change and earnings slow. Take the electric utilities industry in the early 1990s, where many companies were paying out 90 to 100 percent of their earnings in expectations of future earnings growth. The payout ratio was neither sustainable nor realistic. Dividend cuts followed when the earnings didn't materialize.

2. **Current yield relative to industry peers**. Investors should look at the relative yields within an industry group. Often, the industry leader will have a low yield relative to its peers, because investors are willing to pay a premium for a company that has predictable and stronger future earnings growth. At the extreme, an unusually high relative yield signals the market is concerned about fundamentals, either a great opportunity or a potential "terminally cheap" stock. Fundamental research becomes critical in these instances, as previously discussed. Unusually low relative yields compared to industry peers should alert investors to closely examine other valuation metrics. Chances are, a lot of good news is already priced into the stock. Too great a premium suggests that a stock is reaching the range where it is overpriced.

3. **Current yield relative to the firm's average yield over the last five years**. Investors should measure this through the RDY valuation discipline while looking for valuation trends.

4. **The dividend growth rate relative to the earnings growth rate**. These figures provide some signals about a company's future plans, as well as its expectations about the future cost of capital. Declining dividend growth compared to earnings can signal management's

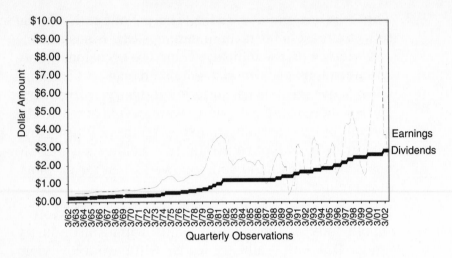

Figure 5.1 Chevron Texaco (CHV) Per Share Dividends and Earnings Comparison
Source: Data from Compustat

expectations for slower growth. Conversely, a dividend growth rate higher than earnings growth can signal management's expectations of accelerated growth in the future. (See Figure 5.1.)

Asset Turnover

Asset turnover measures the ability of the company to extract value out of the assets it has under management. The turnover ratio can be used on a comparative basis to measure the asset utilization rate relative to its peer group and past earnings cycles.

Issues to examine regarding asset turnover include:

1. **Improving or deteriorating asset turns**. It's simple: The faster a company turns over its assets, the greater the profits it can extract for each dollar of assets employed. The rate at which the turnover ratio increases

or decreases gives a partial picture of the future economic health of the company. Asset turnover needs to be looked at in conjunction with capital expenditure (cap-ex) to form a more complete picture, since it is possible to "milk" assets for current earnings rather than investing for the future.

2. **Company turnover ratio relative to the industry turnover ratio**. Relative turnover ratio is another indication of competitive strength. The faster a company turns over assets relative to its competitors, the less it is paying per dollar of revenues and earnings.

3. **Earnings leverage given the turnover ratio relative to the industry average**. To address this, investors should look first at the turnover ratio of comparable companies in the same industry segment to come up with an industry benchmark. They then can look at the company under evaluation and compare it to the benchmark to determine a reasonable earnings level given its current capital structure or asset base. If it is higher than the current earnings level, the question becomes: Is there an additional opportunity to leverage current assets to drive earnings growth?

As an example, an evaluation of EMC in the summer of 2002 showed the current leverage was 0.6. Assuming sales recover and turns (sales/assets) improve to 1, earnings for the company would be $0.55 versus the current earnings per share loss estimate of –0.05. This figure provided confidence that the company had good prospects for improving earnings as it improved its efficiency.

Investment in Business/ROIC

The return on invested capital (ROIC) measures the firm's ability to remain competitive as it reinvests, as well as the marginal contribution of the investments.

Issues to examine regarding investment in business include:

1. **Trend analysis of a firm's ROIC relative to its weighted average cost of capital.** ROIC, expressed as a percentage, can be directly compared to the weighted average cost of capital, which is also a percentage. Investors should expect companies to be able to achieve a return that is consistently higher than the cost of capital, and examine the trend over a moving five-year average.

2. **Cap-ex trends relative to depreciation for the company and the industry.** Although depreciation rates are a product of the tax code, they generally reflect the costs of the replacement of assets within a given industry. Generally, a cap-ex rate in excess of depreciation is a signal that a company is expanding to build its business. Investors should look at those rates not only for individual companies but for the industry as a whole. Among the things they should be on guard against are cap-ex trends that are unsustainable, which occur when an investment cannot be fully depreciated before it must be replaced. The wireless industry has been caught in this trap for a number of years, forced to continually build out its networks, upgrading its technology while at the same time lowering rates to induce more customers to fill the network. The wireless industry's cap-ex needs are enormous, and much of the capital expended by the industry is unlikely to be recovered.

It actually is better to see companies not invest in plant and equipment, when, for instance, there is overcapacity in an industry. A good example of this involves the forest products industry in the late 1990s. Companies like Weyerhaeuser (WY) and International Paper (IP) had overinvested in plants and mills. The overinvestment resulted in too much supply, which increased inventories and put downward pressure on pricing. In this case, lower capital expenditure budgets were viewed positively, and investors were demanding that cap-ex be lower than DD&A to ensure tighter supply and, therefore, strong pricing and profits.

3. **R&D as a percentage of sales historically and relative to industry trends**. New products are the lifeblood of competition, so investors should look at R&D expenditures to gain a better understanding of whether a company is doing enough to remain competitive for the future in the context of its own history and that of its competitors.

Equity Leverage

Equity leverage ties the company's growth objectives to increasing shareholder value. Margins and earnings should improve as the company seeks to grow through acquisitions and expansion.

Issues to examine regarding equity leverage include:

1. **Increasing or decreasing leverage**. Decreasing leverage, which increases share value, even when share prices remain constant, is preferred. Increasing the leverage shifts more of the company's earnings stream into the hands of the debtholders, who permanently remove it from the company, while shareholders receive their payments in the form of dividends, which have the potential for reinvestment.

2. **Earnings growth relative to the growth in leverage**. For this criterion investors should look at earnings growth from the perspective of what is driving the growth. They should understand if acquisitions are potentially masking lackluster growth in the underlying core assets of a company.

3. **Operating margin trends relative to the growth in leverage**. Obviously, it is better to see operating margins rising faster than the growth of leverage. If leverage

is properly deployed in terms of the development of technology, new products, new channels, or new plants, it should pay off through an improvement in operating margins. If it does not, the growth of leverage relative to margins becomes a negative indicator of a company's prospects.

4. **History of write-offs and restructuring charges if growth has been acquisition driven**. Write-offs and restructuring charges are generally a red flag indicator that the company's acquisition philosophy is flawed and shareholder capital is being recklessly wasted. Often, companies are purchased at a premium to their net asset value, which necessitates the booking of Goodwill. If the acquiring company later takes a write-down on the value of the acquired assets or other acquisition-related charges, then this tells investors that the assumptions used to justify the deal price were overly optimistic. Most recently, with the adoption of FASB 142 "Accounting for Goodwill," companies have had to reassess the value of Goodwill booked and take impairment charges as appropriate. Thus, the problem generally comes when a company begins to use acquisitions as its sole growth strategy. In order to finance a string of acquisitions, companies either increase their leverage/debt load, issue more shares, or pay cash. They attempt to maintain or increase share prices by persuading investors that the acquisition will pay off with higher earnings than either company could achieve separately $(1 + 1 = 3)$. As conservative investors, we are cautious about companies that use this as their only strategy for growth.

5. **Trend in the underlying growth rate of the company without acquisitions and relative to the industry**. If a company did not grow by acquisition, would its growth rate still be equal to or greater than its industry? Investors should examine this question by

separating a company's lines of business and divisions into pre- and post-acquisition components, and measuring each rate of growth.

Investors should look for companies that make acquisitions that contribute to the growth of a company's core business, since that represents an addition to the company's overall strength in its markets. Acquisitions that are in unrelated areas carry with them the risk of requiring too much management time, which, while never appearing on the balance sheet, is nevertheless an expense if the acquisition fails to achieve the desired result.

Financial Risk

Financial risk measures the company's debt structure, cost of debt, and ability to administer the debt. On an absolute basis and relative to its peers, this factor seeks to identify companies that unduly leverage their balance sheets to sustain growth.

Issues to examine regarding financial risk include:

1. **Debt/equity ratio adjusted to include off-balance sheet items**. Many companies appear to have a healthier debt/equity ratio than they actually possess. This is because, increasingly, they use off-balance sheet financing to conceal increased debt levels. This is what got Enron in trouble, and could affect many other companies as well. Off-balance sheet financing is difficult to detect precisely because it is off the balance sheet. Investors should try to pinpoint off-balance sheet financing through their research. If they are unable to get a comfortable understanding of what may or may not exist, they should fail the company.

2. **Trend analysis of the coverage ratio**. How much free cash flow is available to cover debt service, growth, and the payment of dividends? Obviously, the higher the ratio over time, the healthier the company.

3. **The firm's reliance on access to the capital markets to fund its growth initiatives**. Investors should view a strong reliance on access to the capital markets as an initial red flag in evaluating potential investments. If a company uses too much debt, the equity investor benefits from the interest tax shield in the short term. However, in the long run, a potential economic or industry slowdown could limit the company's ability to service its debt, which could in turn cause the company to issue more equity and thus dilute the current shareholder base. However, if a company uses equity to raise capital there can also be cause for concern. The concern is that growth may not materialize or could be short lived, with the eventual consequence of equity dilution. Investors should seek companies that can balance internal funding of growth initiatives with funding from the capital markets.

   To put this in context, we failed Calpine on this factor in late 2001. At the time it was evident that the company was reliant upon borrowing to fund its growth. We were concerned that if a credit crunch occurred, the funding strategy would collapse upon itself, and eventually it did.

4. **The firm's historic and projected credit ratings as defined by S&P and Moody's**. A company's cost of borrowing becomes important to investors (and company management) who want to analyze the company's return of capital. When a company is experiencing operating difficulties, credit-rating agencies often put the corporate debt on credit watch or downgrade the debt, resulting in a higher cost of capital for the company.

   If the downgrade results in a rating below investment grade, the combination of the increased cost of capital and the underlying risk should cause investors to be wary, and the company should fail on this factor. A significant downgrade is usually also the precursor to a dividend cut or omission that creates difficulty for investors using RDY as their valuation screen.

5. **The firm's ability to fund or finance any maturing debt and/or puttable bonds over the next twenty-four months**. Access to the credit markets, a sound credit rating, and/or solid cash flow are all required as debt matures. When evaluating this factor, investors should look at a time horizon of two years, since it is difficult to make predictions on the economy or the interest rate environment much past that. They should also consider any convertible bonds, which could potentially dilute equity.

6. **Specific restrictions or covenants stipulated in available credit lines and debt outstanding**. Increasingly, banks are putting restrictions on borrowing, making the debt callable if the shares drop below a certain "trigger" price for a given period of time. Alternatively, companies may be required to maintain sufficiently high coverage ratios in order to be able to have access to their credit lines. Like off-balance sheet financing, these covenants and restrictions can be difficult to discover, so investors have to probe with the corporate finance people to get the disclosure they need to evaluate the true financial health of a company.

CASE STUDY: FINANCIAL RISK FAILURE—EASTMAN KODAK

As an example of a failure on financial risk, here is an excerpt from a 1998 Twelve Fundamental Factor analysis on Eastman Kodak (EK):

After Kodak announced that third quarter 1997 earnings would be below expectations due to weak pricing, a strong dollar, and losses in their digital businesses, the company's debt was put on credit watch with negative implications. While the company has a solid balance sheet, concerns over the fundamental outlook, which may not turn for two more quarters, could result in a debt downgrade from the current (S&P) AA- rating. While management does not believe that a downgrade would impact their cost of borrowing we are taking a conservative stance and failing the company on the financial risk factor.

February 1998

Taking all of these factors into consideration using our evaluation matrix (see page 52), investors are able to systematically evaluate stocks for potential investment. Recapping, investors should require any stock to pass two out of the three qualitative criteria and five out of the nine quantitative criteria to qualify for purchase. We have found this approach provides a good framework for minimizing bad investments. In particular, this discipline helped us minimize losses in companies like JC Penney, *Reader's Digest*, and Eastman Kodak.

A VARIATION ON THE TWELVE FUNDAMENTAL FACTORS—THE BANKING SECTOR

In light of the fact that banking is a fairly unique industry (i.e., one where money taken in is recorded as a liability rather than an asset), we have recently tailored our standard twelve factors approach. When analyzing a bank stock, the qualitative factors are left intact, while five of the nine quantitative factors are changed. For example, factors such as Operating Margins, Cash Flow, and Asset Turnover are not nearly as applicable as Net Interest Margins and Asset Quality due to the fact that banks are in the business of lending and do not produce tangible goods. (Factors changed appear in italics.)

Qualitative (2 of 3)	Y	N	Quantitative (5 of 9)	Y	N
Buggy Whip			Sales/Revenue Growth		
Niche Value			Overhead/Efficiency		
Top Management			Relative P/E		
			Liquidity/Funding Mix		
			Dividend Coverage-Growth		
			Asset Quality		
			Asset-Liability Management		
			Equity Leverage		
			Capital Adequacy		

An explanation of the factors unique to banks follows:

Overhead/Efficiency

In a mature industry such as banking, overhead expense is a critical variable in determining profitability and competitiveness. In terms of profitability, net interest earned and fees collected (or total net revenues) must cover all credit (bad loans) and non-credit (payroll, rents, etc.) related expenses. Thus, controlling overhead is one of the critical ways in which a bank can increase its pre-tax margin. Furthermore, if a bank is a low-cost provider, it is in a better position to compete for loans (i.e., it can charge less interest). Banks with a strong (or improving) expense culture are typically awarded premium (or increasing) valuations as their competitive position is seen to be strong (or strengthening) over time. The critical areas assessed in terms of overhead/efficiency are:

I Level of overhead expenses relative to total net revenues
I Trend in overhead expenses
I Overhead expenses relative to industry

Liquidity/Funding Mix

Because the bulk of a bank's revenues are tied to the interest spread it earns (i.e., the difference between the interest it pays on deposits and the interest it collects on loans), liquidity and funding mix are key determinants of total interest cost. In the simplest example, banks must have enough liquid funds on hand to meet deposit withdrawals and the funding of loans on any given day. By maintaining ample liquidity and a diverse funding mix, a bank ensures that it will not have to pay up for funds at inopportune times. The liquidity/funding mix analysis focuses on:

▌ Historical level and trend in liquidity
▌ Stability of funding mix
▌ Trends in deposit growth relative to industry

Asset Quality

It is often said that when buying a bank stock, an investor is buying a blind pool of risk (i.e., that the true quality of the loan portfolio is unknown to those outside the bank). Furthermore, as our experience in the early 1990s taught us, problem loans are the single biggest wildcard in assessing banks, as they can destroy bank earnings very quickly and in extreme cases, threaten solvency. Therefore, it is critical to review and monitor asset quality as well as understand the bank's approach to managing credit risk (conservative or aggressive, early-identification or late to recognize) before investing. This is not to say that banks should have no bad loans, rather just that they should be pricing appropriately for any risks they take on. To assess asset quality it is important to look at:

▌ Improving or deteriorating asset quality (past-dues and charge-offs)
▌ Loan loss reserve adequacy
▌ Charge-offs relative to loan loss provisions

Asset-Liability Management

Banks must carefully manage the maturity and repricing of their assets and liabilities to ensure against undue interest rate risk. Whether intentional or not, having a significant mismatch between assets and liabilities essentially amounts to a bet on the level and direction of interest rates. Banks that manage this risk conservatively are preferred, as bankers are not paid to speculate on interest rates. Critical issues include:

I   Adequacy of internal tools used to measure, monitor, and assess interest rate risk
I   Level and trend of duration gap or other such measures

Capital Adequacy

Capital or shareholders' equity is the final line of defense against losses for a bank. Regulators attempt to ensure that banks have adequate capital by setting regulatory minimums. Ideally, the level of capital should reflect the level of risk on a bank's balance sheet and beyond (credit, interest rate, off-balance sheet, and operational). Investors can best gauge this by reviewing:

I   The level and trend of capital ratios in relation to regulatory thresholds and minimums
I   Make-up of the capital base (tangible versus intangible)
I   Share repurchase activity

NOTES

1. Jim Collins, *Good to Great* (New York: Harper Collins Publisher Inc., 2001), p. 10.
2. Microsoft Investor Strategy Lab, Value Seeker Journal: April 17, 1998, www.investor.msn.com 5/12/98.

6

RDY CASE STUDIES

*"In this game, the market has to keep pitching, but you don't
have to swing. You can stand there with the bat on your
shoulder for six months until you get a fat pitch."*

Warren Buffett

The previous chapters described two methodologies, RDY and
RPSR, for valuing stocks. To give context, this chapter provides
some examples of how RDY can be put into practice. Throughout these case studies, various examples of returns (total
return) on investments signaled by RDY are given to show the
potential results of this investment approach (for consistency,
the last business day of the month is used for the buy or sell
transaction). You will notice that, in many cases, RDY is clearly
a long-term investing strategy, as it can take an average of one
to three years or more for a company to move from the buy
range to the sell range. Chapter 7 will discuss examples of RPSR
and the relationship between RDY and RPSR when both
methodologies can be applied to the same stock.

Note: This chapter contains examples of stocks we have
owned at one point or another in portfolios we managed for
institutional and private clients. When looking at the RDY
charts, it is important to note that they reflect monthly data

points. Stocks may cross into and out of the buy or sell range on an intra-month basis. For clarity of presentation, monthly data is used. All returns represent total returns including capital appreciation and any dividends paid during the period.

OIL STOCKS

Exxon Mobil

Oil stocks generally are classic representations of how RDY can be applied to generate returns in excess of the market over time. Exxon Mobil provides an excellent real-world example. The RDY charts for oil stocks illustrate how changes in the price and perceived availability of oil affect the relative attractiveness of a stock in this group. On the Exxon chart (Figure 6.1), Area A highlights the two energy crises of the 1970s, which, between them, moved the price of oil from $3 per barrel in 1970 to $34 per barrel in 1981. Area B shows the impact of the Gulf War and political unrest in the Middle East, which drove up oil prices and, in turn, pushed Exxon's stock into the sell range. Area C illustrates an unusual time for Exxon in which it was influenced

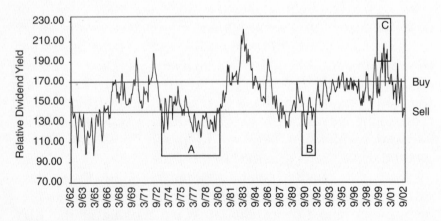

Figure 6.1   Exxon Mobil Corp. (XOM) Relative Dividend Yield
Source: Data from Compustat.

both by declining oil prices and by the movement of investor capital to the technology sector.

To show the value of RDY for this type of stock, it is interesting to look at the potential results of a buy and sell as indicated by the charts. For instance, if an investor purchased Exxon at the month-end of February 1981 when it entered the buy range, and then sold it at the end of April 1987, when it entered the sell range, the return for the period would have been 288.1 percent for Exxon, compared to 190.3 percent for the S&P 500.

When looking at RDY, it is important to remember why this investment approach works—the stability of the dividend and the deliberateness of the approach that a corporate Board of Directors employs in setting the dividend. Figure 6.2 shows the relationship between dividends and earnings for Exxon. The company has maintained a steady dividend policy over time, although earnings have fluctuated, clearly showing that dividend growth is a normalized indicator of earnings growth. One can see that in the 1999 to 2000 time frame the company raised the dividend in anticipation of rising earnings.

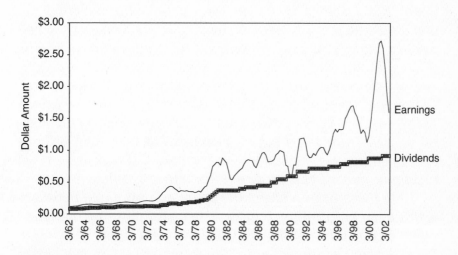

Figure 6.2 Exxon Mobil Corp. (XOM) Per Share Dividends and Earnings Comparison
Source: Data from Compustat.

PHARMACEUTICAL STOCKS

Wyeth (WYE) (formerly American Home Products)

Wyeth (WYE) is a global company with a history of strong research and pharmaceutical product development. In reflecting on this stock, it is interesting to look at the late 1990s. In 1997, the company came into the buy range, driven by the "fen-phen" furor, which led to questions about potential liability as well as the company's ability to grow through the sale of other products. At the time, our research showed that this was a temporary event that was not of concern to long-term investors.

In March 1998, WYE (at that time American Home Products) was left standing at the alter (while its potential mate, Smith Kline Beecham (SBH), skipped off with its new betrothed—Glaxo-Wellcome). Speculation was that the merger had failed because the two companies couldn't come to terms with WYE's diet drug liability or could not agree on who would run the combined company. The stock declined about $6—giving value investors a chance to buy. At the time that the SBH talks with WYE were disclosed, WYE was already among the cheapest stocks in the pharmaceutical industry due to its recall of Redux and Pondimin diet drugs the previous year. To make matters worse, WYE then disclosed that the company was going to withdraw one of its new drugs (Verdia) for hypertension. Verdia was under FDA review, and a *Wall Street Journal* report stated that insiders had sold shares after the stock surged in late January. As shown by Area A of Figure 6.3, WYE was clearly in the RDY buy range. Fundamental analysis revealed a strong management team and balance sheet, impressive earnings (even without the drugs in the pipeline), and one of the lowest P/Es in the industry.

If an investor purchased the stock at month-end February 1998 (even before the stock was hit with news of the failed merger), and then subsequently sold when it crossed back into the sell range in September of the same year, he or she would have seen the stock price go from $47 to $53 over the course of five months. This corresponds to a 13.3 percent return over the same period, compared to an S&P 500 return of -2.2 percent.

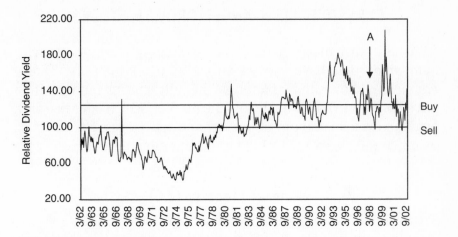

Figure 6.3 Wyeth (WYE) Relative Dividend Yield
Source: Data from Compustat.

For illustration purposes, we have included a dividend versus earnings chart for WYE shown in Figure 6.4. Like other companies, its history shows a pattern of deliberate dividend policies in the face of changing earnings.

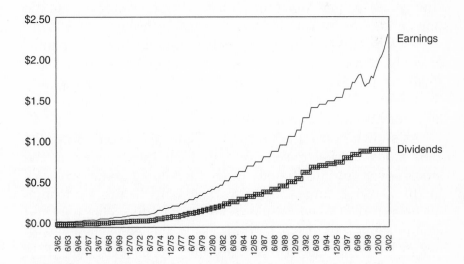

Figure 6.4 Wyeth (WYE) Per Share Dividends and Earnings Comparison
Source: Data from Compustat.

CLASSIC FALLEN-ANGEL GROWTH STOCKS

RDY is particularly useful in evaluating former growth companies that have moved into a state of maturity. These companies show similar patterns—initially starting out with Relative Dividend Yields well below the market, which later rise and begin to cycle in and out of the buy and sell ranges. For another example see pages 147 to 149 for a discussion of Coke.

General Electric (GE)

From an RDY perspective, General Electric (GE) is a classic growth company. From 1962 until just recently, GE stayed out of the buy range, as it turned in year-after-year of solid earnings growth. Even though its dividend growth continued to rise by double digits for more than fifteen years, the company remained out of reach for value investors whose discipline included a focus on above-market dividend yields. GE recently came into the buy range for the first time as a confluence of factors created the "perfect storm" and eroded investor sentiment on the stock. Jack Welch stepped down as CEO, the Honeywell acquisition failed, orders were cancelled in the power sector as the industry worked through short-term excess supply issues, investors became skeptical of companies growing through acquisitions, the economy slowed, and, finally, a renowned bond manager criticized the company's financing policy. All these factors contributed to short-term investor disenchantment with GE.

As shown in the RDY chart in Figure 6.5, even during the 1987 stock market correction and 1990–1991 recession, the stock never got into the buy range (as highlighted in Area A). In these trying times, investors had faith in the company's business model—acquisitions combined with productivity and quality gains—to drive margins, plus the consistency with which GE Financial would continue to deliver quality EPS growth. This business model has not changed. Since GE has

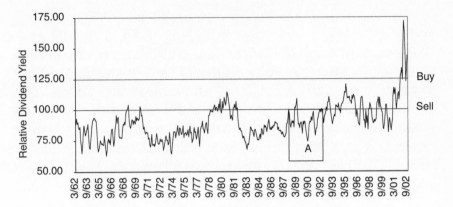

Figure 6.5 General Electric Corp. (GE) Relative Dividend Yield
Source: Data from Compustat.

been a large part of the S&P 500 Index growth, investors in the recent past have overweighted the stock, expecting the 28 percent annualized return from 1990–2000, which surpassed the market's 15.4 percent annual return, to continue to contribute positively to their portfolio's performance. In light of the events previously described and the fact that large cap growth investing is currently out of favor, these same investors are paring back their overweight positions, further exacerbating the stock's decline. We believe this will be a great opportunity to invest in an exceptionally well-run company with good underlying business fundamentals. If history is any guide, GE should become a resounding investment success, although not in the short term.

3M (MMM)

3M (MMM) is a quality fallen-angel growth company which has historically produced a broad range of profitable products by leveraging its technological and "go-to-market" capabilities across product categories. Although known to most consumers through its brands such as Scotch Tape and Post-it Notes, the company manufactures items ranging from reflecting materials for highway marking to health care products. In the late 1960s and early 1970s, it was one of the Nifty Fifty growth stocks. While many of those stocks languished after a downturn in 1973 and 1974, MMM recovered because of its demonstrated ability to turn out an endless stream of profitable new products. The company maintained strong growth throughout the 1980s. As highlighted in Area A in Figure 6.6, MMM first came into the buy range in March 1994, after just missing the buy range in the early 1990s. The company moved into fallen-angel status due to a number of factors:

I In the mid-1990s the company ran into "problems" with earnings, due to a combination of circumstances including a somewhat "overweight" cost structure, the need to rationalize some business lines, and unfavorable currency translation. Unfortunately, the market had become accustomed to very predictable earnings from MMM. When the company disappointed, the market quickly lost faith in it.

I Additionally, investor focus on technology-oriented companies resulted in a loss of constituency for MMM.

In 2000, the company's CEO, Mr. DeSimone, retired, and former GE executive W. James McNerney, Jr., was brought in to add a bit of General Electric-style aggressiveness in terms of business focus and management. McNerney restructured the company and its performance improved, helping to push the stock higher and the RDY down, although it remained buyable. The company also decided to stop manufacturing Scotchgard products, to avoid creating future liability, after it learned that a compound used in manufacturing the product was "persistent and pervasive" in the environment and human blood streams. It also began acquiring advanced technology components of other companies that fit into its business plan. These included Polaroid's Technical Polarizer and Display Films business, and Hoechst's share of a fluorine elastomer joint venture MMM had entered into with Hoechst. McNerney has continued

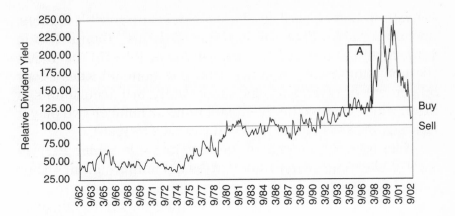

Figure 6.6 3M (MMM) Relative Dividend Yield
Source: Data from Compustat.

to streamline the company and brought a more aggressive leadership style to the organization. We expect his efforts to continue to pay off and move the stock back into the sell range.

If an investor had purchased the stock when it entered the buy range in March 1994 (assume a purchase date of 3/30/94), and held on to it until September 30, 2002, it would have returned 189.0 percent versus 112.7 percent for the S&P 500 over the same period. This is a particularly attractive result given the continuing bear market and considering the stock has still not hit the sell line.

CONSUMER STOCKS

Gillette (G)

Gillette (G) traces its roots back to the turn of the century when King Gillette, a salesman, came up with the idea of disposable blades. While shaving has been its core business ever since, the company's marginal growth has increasingly been driven by acquisitions in other consumer product areas. For example, from 1960 to 1990, much of the company's growth came from Right Guard deodorant, Cricket disposable lighters, and Eraser Mate Pens (all in the early 1960s), then Braun in 1967, Liquid Paper in 1979, and Oral-B in 1984. In the 1990s, the company greatly increased its international sales—now 60 percent of revenues—and made additional acquisitions in areas where it could be the number one or number two player (such as Parker Pens in 1993 and Duracell in 1996).

Gillette stock eventually became buyable under RDY in 1999 as slower growth resulted in disappointing earnings. (See Area A in Figure 6.7.) Driving the negative trends were poor conditions in international markets (due mostly to currency devaluations in Russia and Brazil), underperformance in the company's stationery unit (Paper Mate, Parker Pens, Water-man, and Liquid Paper), and the fact that G was not a high-flying technology stock. This led to a multi-year stretch of corporate reorganizations, cost cutting, and management transition. Michael Hawley became CEO in 1999, but was fired in late 2000; the company operated under an acting CEO until eventually hiring former Nabisco President James Kilts in February 2001. The recent appreciation in G stock has been driven by a

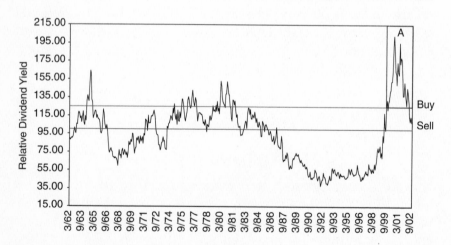

Figure 6.7   Gillette (G) Relative Dividend Yield
Source: Data from Compustat.

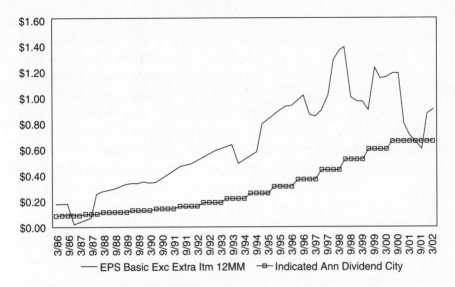

Figure 6.8 Gillette (G) Per Share Dividends and Earnings Comparison
Source: Data from Compustat.

combination of new management, progress on reducing costs, a growing appreciation for defensive stocks, and finally, evidence of a long-awaited turnaround in sales and earnings growth. (See Figure 6.8.)

The company entered the buy range in September 1999. If an investor held onto the stock through September 30, 2002 (when the stock had not yet reached the sell range), the returns on G would have been −0.1 percent compared to −41.6 percent for the S&P 500.

Kimberly-Clark (KMB)

One thing most analysts agree on is that Kimberly-Clark (KMB) is the innovation leader within the personal care paper goods industry. KMB had been a fully integrated paper products company until an important strategic decision was made to divest the paper mills and focus on consumer products and health care. The company's weakness in the mid-1990s was prompted by difficulties in integrating its 1995 acquisition of Scott Paper. After the Scott Paper acquisition, the stock appreciated into the sell range based on our Relative Dividend Yield valuation methodology. By late 1997 and early 1998, four consecutive quarters of earnings disappointments, due largely to pricing pressures, moved the stock back into the buy range. Management announced a series of restructuring charges for layoffs and facilities closures. As shown in Area A of Figure 6.9, just as investors might start to consider purchase of the stock in spring 1998, the company disappointed investors again, driving KMB into a prolonged stay in the buy range. This time poor revenue growth in Europe due to overcapacity in tissue production, weak pulp pricing, and the ongoing diaper wars for market share with Procter & Gamble pressured the stock. Chairman Wayne Sanders faced an incredulous Wall Street and the stock sold off to the high $30s. Sanders restructured the company, selling off many of the company's timber and timber-related interests, and reinvesting the money in higher-margin medical supply businesses. At the same time, the company moved strongly into the Asian market. This led to strong earnings gains, but just as important, sharp increases in income as a percent of sales.[1]

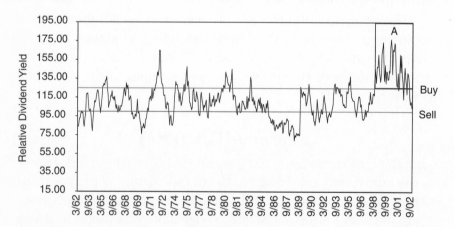

Figure 6.9   Kimberly-Clark (KMB) Relative Dividend Yield
Source: Data from Compustat.

Investing in the company when it entered the buy range in March 1998 and holding onto it until September 30, 2002 (when the stock had yet to reach the sell line) would have resulted in a 23.2 percent return for KMB versus a −21.4 percent return for the S&P 500.

BANK STOCKS/FINANCIALS

Wells Fargo (WFC)

After a nice run in the late 1960s and early 1970s, Wells Fargo (WFC) struggled and finally succumbed to the many macroeconomic factors that were causing instability for U.S. banks during that period (introduction of floating exchange rates, spiking oil prices, high inflation, and wild swings in interest rates). The downtrend that started in 1973, which ultimately caused the stock to become buyable under RDY, lasted through the double-dip 1980–1982 recession.

It wasn't until 1985 that investor sentiment toward banks became positive again. It became increasingly clear that the favorable macroeconomic environment (economic growth, slowing inflation, and declining interest rates and unemployment) was creating somewhat of a tailwind for the banks.

As we know from hindsight those good times ultimately ended with the 1990 recession, a time when banks were still heavily involved in lending to real estate developers based on ever-optimistic future economic growth and demand projections (not to mention highly inflated real estate prices). Suffering under the weight of a concentrated California real estate portfolio, WFC again became buyable for a brief period in 1990 as highlighted in Area A in Figure 6.10.

The final and wildest swing in WFC's chart came as the RDY rose to an all-time high of over twice that of the market (see Area B). Investors threw out banks as "old economy" slow-growth stocks, instead favoring high-growth "new

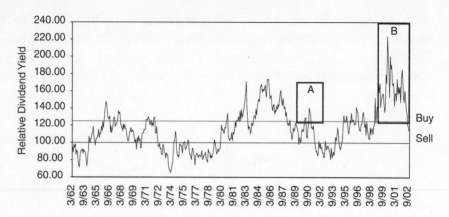

Figure 6.10 Wells Fargo (WFC) Relative Dividend Yield
Source: Data from Compustat.

economy" Internet and technology stocks. While the stock has since recovered, its current yield of 1.14 times the market tells us that it still has some room to run.

The returns on an investment in WFC stock would be quite attractive. For instance, investing in November 1994 when the company rose out of the sell range and into the buy range, then selling approximately three years later in December 1997 when the yield almost reached the sell range again, would earn a 286.0 percent return. The return for the S&P 500 was 128.8 percent. If an investor held onto the stock until there was a clear sell indicator (there has not been one at month-end since 1994), the return through September 30, 2002, would have been 429.2 percent versus 105.0 percent for the S&P 500. Following the RDY guideline for this stock has resulted in a buy and hold strategy for this stock that has to date produced a spectacular result.

Marsh & McLennan (MMC)

Throughout much of its history, Marsh & McLennan Companies (MMC) has been an acquisition-driven growth story within the mature and cyclical insurance brokerage industry (it is also in two other businesses: benefits consulting through Mercer and investment management/mutual funds through Putnam).

The property and casualty insurance industry (both insurers and brokerages) has been consolidating in the face of overcapacity for many years. MMC had the good fortune to be at the forefront of this trend and became one of only a few insurance brokers that has the scale necessary to place the risks of today's complex global corporations.

As Figure 6.11 depicts, MMC did not enter the buy range until 1980. During the preceding period, the company pursued its insurance brokerage business in an environment characterized by a long period of soft insurance market conditions. During that period, insurance companies were aggressively undercutting each other in an effort to maintain market share. Although as a broker, MMC was somewhat insulated from these price wars, declining premiums were ultimately reflected in declining commissions for the company. This was the primary factor for the loss of favor for the stock and ultimately its progress into the buy range under RDY in 1980. After a series of consolidations enabled the industry to

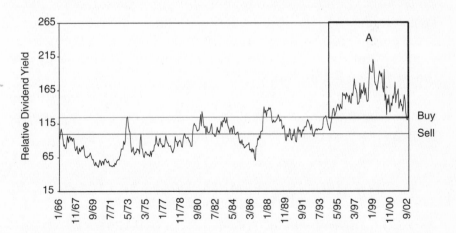

Figure 6.11 Marsh & McLennan (MMC) Relative Dividend Yield
Source: Data from Compustat.

price more aggressively, MMC was in prime position to ride the wave of skyrocketing insurance prices that occurred from 1984 to 1986 and move back into the sell range.

Unfortunately, that up cycle in insurance pricing proved to be brief as the insurer's windfall attracted new entrants that drove insurance pricing downward—a trend that lasted through the late 1990s. While MMC became increasingly buyable during the decade of the 1990s (see Area A), the most recent upward revaluation (or decline in its RDY) occurred as its investment management subsidiary, Putnam, rode the heady bull market of the late 1990s.

In the midst of a twenty-six-month bear market and poor business conditions, MMC has been in a trading range as investors weigh the near- and long-term growth prospects of Putnam and the consulting business.

Once Marsh & McLennan's RDY reached the buy range in June 1987, an investor who bought then would stand to receive a 46.1 percent return if he or she sold the stock when it dipped below the sell range in October 1989. The S&P 500 return for the same period was 21.3 percent.

If an investor bought the stock again when it entered the buy range in December 1993 and held on until September 30, 2002 (when it had not yet hit the sell range), he or she would have a 290.2 percent return versus 104.6 percent for the S&P 500, while enjoying substantial, above-market dividend increases along the way. (See Figure 6.12.)

These stocks may not be exciting, as they sometimes seem to be moving at glacial speed. However, for the patient investor, excess return is obtained time and time again.

RDY FAILURES—TERMINALLY CHEAP STOCKS

As with any investment discipline, there are stocks for which the discipline does not work. For RDY, one of the biggest potential pitfalls is buying and holding onto terminally cheap stocks or cyclical stocks that will never move back into the sell range.

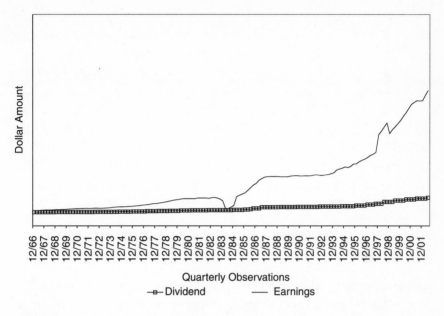

Figure 6.12 Marsh & McLennan (MMC) Per Share Dividends and Earnings Comparison
Source: Data from Compustat.

Verizon (VZ)

Verizon (VZ) provides an interesting example of an RDY company that has been in the buy range for an extended period of time. VZ is the result of Bell Atlantic's merger with NYNEX and the subsequent merger of the combined companies with GTE. Like other Regional Bell Operating Companies (RBOCs), the company's share price in the early years following its separation from AT&T tended to be negatively correlated to interest rates. As time passed and the true nature of the less-regulated telecommunications services business became clearer, these stocks became more sensitive to overall economic conditions (the stocks showed a more moderated cyclical pattern compared to a traditional cyclical stock.) Overall, VZ's generally steady earnings and growth, as well as its attractive yield compared to the rest of the market, have provided the *characteristics* of a potentially attractive investment. VZ has maintained a consistent

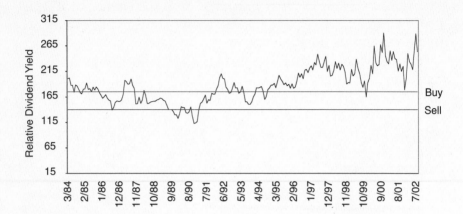

Figure 6.13 Verizon Communications (VZ) Relative Dividend Yield
Source: Data from Compustat.

dividend policy, enabling it to provide an above-market yield. The stock has recently been trading at a little over two times the market yield. On a yield basis this is attractive; however, on an RDY basis we seek stocks that are driven into their sell ranges by the marketplace. (See Figure 6.13.)

VZ is a stock that started a long-term secular trend up in its RDY. Any long-term secular rise or fall in RDY results in the discipline no longer working. In the case of secular up trends, one never reaches the sell indicator. In the case of secular down trends one never reaches the buy indicator.

As validation of why RDY does not work in this case, an investment in VZ in December 1991, when RDY signaled a buy, would have returned only 74.9 percent compared to 142.3 percent for the S&P 500 as of September 30, 2002. In other words, there are plenty of other better places to invest.

Heinz (HNZ) (More than just a little slow out of the bottle—this stock is terminally cheap)

For many years we justified our holding in Heinz (HZ) as well-placed, if not a little early. As the years passed we had to acknowledge that we were not only early but wrong. With a disciplined valuation approach and the benefit of our proprietary Twelve Fundamental Factors, we do not often find ourselves in this position.

As shown in Figure 6.14, the stock first entered into the buy range in 1993. A growth stock for the previous thirty years, the RDY rose to a level that was attractive, which prompted a look at the company fundamentals of this classic fallen angel. The company passed the Twelve Fundamental Factors handily, although we had reservations about the Board. It was a nineteen-member "insider" Board that was clearly the handiwork of Tony O'Reilly, the charismatic, legendary CEO of Heinz during the growth heydays. (See pages 59–60 for a more detailed discussion of this aspect of Heinz.)

The company announced a restructuring program in February 1997, as well as the succession of William Johnson as CEO following Tony O'Reilly's retirement in 1998. Investors were enthusiastic about the restructuring, believing it would improve margins and marketing support for some of the company's strongest brands, thereby enhancing revenue growth. In addition, Johnson was perceived as a no-nonsense manager

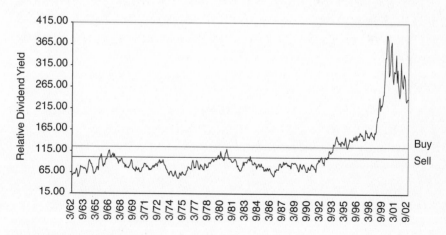

Figure 6.14 Heinz Co. (HNZ) Relative Dividend Yield
Source: Data from Compustat.

who would focus on the top and bottom line. The stock outperformed in the ensuing months but fell off after one disappointment followed another.

Johnson and the stock struggled as first tuna, then ketchup, then pet food and tuna again faced slowing growth, price wars, and rising commodity prices. Just as one segment would improve, another would falter, resulting in stagnant growth in the top line and pressure on the bottom line. Each explanation was reasonable and each proposed solution seemed appropriate. We reassessed the Twelve Fundamental Factors a number of times, but the company still passed, and the valuation simply became more attractive according to our RDY discipline.

However, the stock got cheaper and cheaper. Relative to the market, the stock has provided some protection over the last two years, but that is what is called a Pyrrhic victory. Recently, the company announced another restructuring and divestiture.

HZ is a perfect example of a terminally cheap stock. Discipline and valuation did not matter. Despite our best efforts, during times like these we simply have to say "uncle."

In the case of Heinz, an investment in September 1993, when the stock reached the buy indicator would have resulted in a 90.8 percent return versus 109.4 percent for the S&P 500 as of September 2002 (the stock has yet to move out of the buy range.)

NOTES

1. Kimberly-Clark is discussed at length in Jim Collins' analysis of business success, *Good to Great*. See especially pages 59–62.

7

RPSR CASE STUDIES

"It's either the warning bell or the dinner bell."

Walter Wilson

This chapter examines stocks that are evaluated with a Relative Price-to-Sales Ratio (RPSR) methodology. Most of these stocks would be classified as growth stocks, in that they pay either no dividend or a dividend that is insignificant to the investment decision. Many of these stocks have sold at very high relative price-to-sales ratios for extended periods, and have now fallen to more attractive levels. The question is, does a decline of RPSR signal the same kind of buying opportunity that a rising dividend yield does? The charts and our experience, we believe, show that an RPSR decline can be used as the basis for a value-oriented buy and sell discipline, even though there is no dividend to reward investors. Why? Because the price an investor pays for a unit of sales is a compelling and reliable indicator of value, and sales are, generally speaking, one of the most reliable financial characteristics. It is true that sales can be manipulated, but this is the exception, not the norm. (Some of the recent high profile exceptions included

Bristol-Myers Squibb, which persuaded vendors to take excess inventory so it could book sales in advance, and left shareholders paying the price. Companies such as Enron have made no-profit swap sales with other utilities to inflate their revenues, and been caught. Obviously, sales can be manipulated, but such fraudulent practices are generally rare.)

For the purposes of illustration, this chapter provides some examples of the theoretical results of buys and sells as indicated by RPSR. To simplify the analysis for these examples, the transactions are assumed to take place on the last day of the month. This method provides a good baseline for returns, although we generally take a more gradual "average in, average out" approach.

Note: At some point in time we have had positions in each of these stocks in client portfolios. When looking at the RPSR charts, it is important to note that they reflect monthly data points. Stocks may cross into and out of the buy or sell range on an intra-month basis. For clarity of presentation, monthly data is used. All returns represent total returns.

RPSR AND THE TECHNOLOGY BUBBLE

Given the recent implosion of the technology bubble, it seems timely to start this chapter by looking at what RPSR told us during the tech bubble. At the height of the dotcom mania, we didn't manage to make the incredible returns other firms were temporarily earning from investing in fast-moving initial public offerings (IPOs). But then again, we did not get burned when the dotcom bubble burst. RPSR led the disciplined investor into high quality technology stocks that generated healthy returns, but could not provide valuable insight into emergency technology or Internet-related companies. One of the fail safe attributes of RPSR is that a reasonable sales history is required to set statistically correct buy and sell ranges. This kept us from chasing the latest fad.

Intel (INTC)

Intel (INTC) would ordinarily be the kind of company that would never appear in a value investor's portfolio. It did not even pay a dividend until 1992. As the company that invented the microprocessor, INTC has been a driving force of the productivity enhanced technology boom. Yet, the RPSR has been highly cyclical, providing investors with numerous opportunities to buy and sell the stock. The stock and the company's fortunes are driven largely by the company's new product introduction cycle. When a new generation of processors is introduced, prices are high. As competitor clones begin to appear and the product cycle lengthens, price falls rapidly, and INTC makes its earnings up on rising volume. However, the end of each cycle creates pressure on earnings resulting in a dip into the buy range. In 1988, 1991, and 1995 to 1996, INTC moved into RPSR buy territory, providing value investors with the opportunity to invest in what is unquestionably the world's leading semiconductor maker.

In addition to the new product introduction cycle, INTC (and many technology companies) is affected by the cycles of economic growth. Investors forgot that technology stocks were cyclical growth stocks in the 1990s and held on too long. RPSR was a powerful indicator of overvaluation during the period and gave investors a discipline to get out despite the hype and the cries that it was "different this time."

In terms of RPSR, one of the most interesting periods for INTC (highlighted in Area A of Figure 7.1) was late 1999 to early 2000. Over this period, INTC moved into the RPSR sell range for a prolonged period of time, with an RPSR of 7.5 times sales, far above INTC's normal range and an unsustainable level if history was any guide—for those valuations to make sense, the world would have had to change dramatically. We took this opportunity to take profits with the expectation of having an opportunity to reinvest later at more attractive valuations.

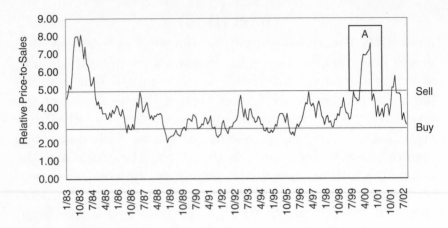

Figure 7.1   Intel Corp. (INTC) Relative Price-to-Sales Ratio
Source: Data from Compustat.

Investors following RPSR who bought at month-end December 1995, when INTC crossed into the buy range, and then sold when it crossed through the sell range in January 2000 would have bought at $14.19 and sold at $98.94 for a 602.2 percent gain. The return on the S&P 500 for the same period was only 142.3 percent.

Estee Lauder (EL)

Estee Lauder (EL) is one of our newer RPSR investments, having been added to our portfolios for the first time in early 2002. Although the stock had a shorter history than we typically like to see, we immediately took notice of the ideal pattern exhibited in the RPSR chart. As shown in Figure 7.2, in just six short years, the stock cycled through its buy–sell range nearly three times. Moreover, despite its short history as a public company, EL is actually very well-established, having been around since the 1940s, with an experienced management team.

The Estee Lauder of today is a global powerhouse in cosmetics, skin care, and fragrance and has built a stable of

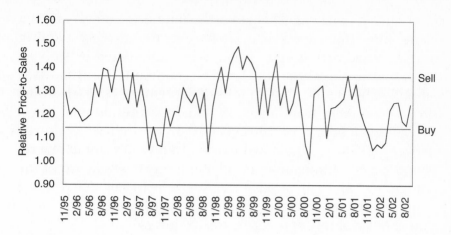

Figure 7.2 Estee Lauder Companies Inc.—Class A (EL) Relative Price-to-Sales Ratio
Source: Data from Compustat.

sixteen leading brands. Management is highly regarded for their ability to create and manage unique brands that make a real connection with consumers (i.e., Clinique as a scientifically advanced skin care brand and M.A.C. as one that appeals to a hipper, edgier crowd). Perhaps as important, the company is also a leader in terms of innovation, which is critical to driving sustained sales growth. In terms of distribution, the company has responded adeptly to the changes in consumers' cosmetics purchasing behavior. Recognizing the declining appeal of big department stores, the company has been supplementing its distribution model with company-owned stores for its smaller specialty lines, such as M.A.C., Aveda, and Origins. The company has also been using the Internet to broaden its reach and to respond to today's more hectic lifestyle (for example, convenient replenishment purchases for busy women and better targeting of new product trial offers).

Some of these moves have been looked upon with skepticism by investors who say the company risks cannibalization of its department store sales and/or it will upset its major distribution partners. This is partly behind the stock's recent cycle into the buy range; however, the driving catalyst into the most recent buy opportunity was created by slowing sales due to the slump in the U.S. economy. The trend was amplified by the terrorist attacks of September 11, 2001, which drove customers from malls. In addition, international travel (a significant source of sales via duty-free purchasing) slowed drastically. The recent slowdown said a lot more about macroeconomic conditions than it did about any degradation of the company's competitive position. Needless to say, this revenue and earnings momentum can be easily restored as consumption and travel return to more normal levels.

In fact, an investor following RPSR, buying at month-end January 2001, when the stock moved into the buy range, and then selling in September 2002 would have seen a return 14.9 percent greater than the S&P 500 Index (−23.9 percent for EL versus −38.8 percent for the S&P 500).

Microsoft (MSFT)

Microsoft (MSFT) is the quintessential growth company. Its domination of the desktop software market was so complete it attracted the attention of the Justice Department. The stock in the past has generally traded with PC fundamentals since a large portion of its revenues are PC driven. Lately, however, in addition to the weak PC fundamentals, the company's legal woes, namely anticompetitive lawsuits brought forth by the Justice Department and various states' Attorney Generals as well as competitors and the European Union (EU) have weighed on the stock's valuation. The case near term that is expected to have the biggest impact on the stock is the Department of Justice (DOJ) case. That case was settled with half of the eighteen states filing suit, and the DOJ. However, the courts must now approve the settlement over the opposition of the remaining states. Meanwhile, MSFT's latest version of Windows has met with only lukewarm response in the marketplace, and consumers have not shown any inclination to increase PC purchases. To broaden its revenue base, the company is slowly moving into other high-margin areas, such as enterprise software. Nonetheless, its current annual sales growth of 12 percent, while still robust, is nowhere near its historical rates, which approached 33 percent annually. In addition, the company's core rate of growth in the enterprise software and services segment slowed down to 7 percent year-over-year growth, as PC sales continued to be mired in a slump. The company's margins were also impacted in the past twelve months as the sales slowdown, investment in new initiatives, and decelerating economic environment impacted the company. This has caused MSFT to recently dip again into our buy range (see Area A in Figure 7.3)

Using RPSR, an investor buying MSFT in December 1995 would have earned a 176.9 percent return if it was sold once the stock entered the sell range in April 1997. This compares to a 33.8 percent return for the S&P 500 over the same time frame.

Figure 7.3 Microsoft Corp. (MSFT) Relative Price-to-Sales Ratio
Source: Data from Compustat.

More recently, if an investor had purchased the stock in December 2000, and then held onto the stock through September 30, 2002 (the stock has not yet reached the sell range), returns would have been 0.8 percent for MSFT versus −36.7 percent for the market.

Oracle (ORCL)

Oracle (ORCL) is a leader in the systems software industry, and is the dominant player in the database market. ORCL's chart in Figure 7.4 reflects in some part the cycles of the economy, including the 1990–1991 recession (Area A), the 1998 Asian crisis (Area B), Y2K, and most recently the Internet bubble. The current economic slowdown is again creating a potential buying opportunity like prior periods. The company has been aggressive in cutting costs and marketing its applications business, its next growth driver to supplant the slow growth of the database business.

ORCL is another good example of how RPSR works. An investor who bought the stock when RPSR indicated a buy in

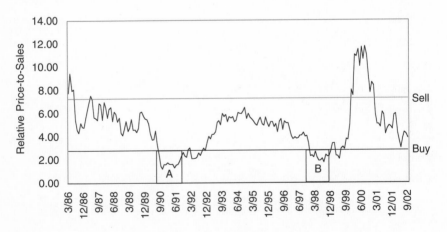

Figure 7.4   Oracle Corporation (ORCL) Relative Price-to-Sales Ratio
Source: Data from Compustat.

December 1997, and then later sold in December 1999 when RPSR indicated a sell, would have had a 653.4 percent gain on the stock versus a 55.6 percent gain for the S&P 500.

The Walt Disney Company (DIS)

The Walt Disney Company (DIS), with its diverse movies, broadcasting, Internet, and theme park operations, is the second-largest media and entertainment conglomerate in the world. The past five years have not been kind to DIS due to investor focus on new economy stocks, lackluster growth at the ABC television network, a period of overinvestment as the company expanded its theme parks, the September 11 terrorist attacks, an overall weak economy, and mixed results in movie releases. All of these factors have resulted in a declining RPSR over the past several years (highlighted with an arrow in Figure 7.5) and a potential opportunity for value investors.

While sales have doubled since DIS's 1996 acquisition of the ABC television network, more than $1 billion of annual profit has evaporated, and income as a percentage of sales, once

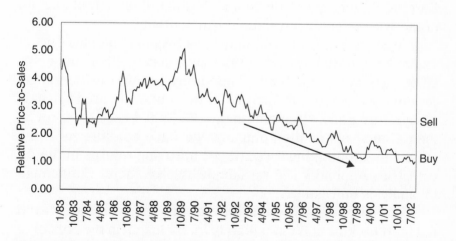

Figure 7.5 The Walt Disney Company (DIS) Relative Price-to-Sales Ratio
Source: Data from Compustat.

a healthy 10 percent, is now below 5 percent. Just as DIS finished a huge expansion at its California theme park and was finishing major additions at Orlando, the economy turned sour, and then the September 11 terrorist attacks turned off the tourist spigot. Meanwhile, the ripple effect of the economy was also felt throughout the advertising industry, which along with a weak program lineup negatively impacted ABC's top and bottom line. Moreover, weak performance of Disney movies at the box office has added to the weakness.

DIS has also been plagued by some high profile missteps. The company's venture into the Internet, the GO network—a joint venture of Infoseek and Disney—quickly faltered and was dissolved in 2001. DIS then got into a bruising fight with Time Warner Cable, which led to ABC being taken off the air to 3.5 million cable households during the all-important sweeps period in 2000. In addition, ABC has been persistently rejiggered and restructured, as it tries to find a winning lineup of shows.

However, the company now is focused on generating above-average returns by reducing debt, right-sizing divisions that have generated sub-par returns (such as ABC, Studio Entertainment, and Consumer Products), and building its brand with selective investments in content.

Purchasing stock in DIS may have been a good idea once it entered the RPSR buy range in May 1999, but as of September 30, 2002, the stock has actually dipped further into the buy range, producing a negative return of 46.7 percent, compared to a negative return of 34.6 percent on the S&P 500. Based on a fundamental analysis of the company, we have confidence in the stock and are looking forward to improving returns in the future. (See Appendix D for a sample Twelve Factor Fundamental analysis on Disney.)

Note: Although DIS came into the buy range in 1999, we did not start looking at it immediately for inclusion in the portfolio. We completed our fundamental analysis and waited to purchase the stock until 2001 when we had a more favorable cost basis. It's important to note that when a stock comes into the buy range for the first time, a great deal of care must be taken to complete the fundamental analysis. No purchase should be made until there is a high level of conviction in the long-term prospects of the stock. In the past we have bought a stock when it entered the buy range for the first time and later found out we bought too soon.

EMC (EMC)

EMC, the dominant company in data storage technology, has grown faster than the information economy, as spending on storage capacity and management outpaced spending in other technology related sectors. Its earliest products were directed at large IBM computers, when mainframes dominated the computer market. In the early 1990s, however, with the advent of smaller client server technology, EMC moved into that market with its Centriplex products. As the computer market began to migrate to the Internet, EMC moved quickly in that direction as well, invading the data switching and computer connection markets in 1995 with the acquisition of McData, which it has since spun off to shareholders. In 1997, as many companies moved their data to the Internet, the company entered into the data site management business, both domestically and internationally. They then went further down market and, anticipating an explosion in Internet enterprise, purchased Data General in 1999.

With the collapse of the Internet bubble, EMC stock suffered, and the company moved into the buy range on an RPSR basis (Area A of Figure 7.6 highlights the company's rise and fall during the technology boom and subsequent bust). The current cycle has one added twist—increased competition—which has eroded the company's pricing power and margins. However, the company, as it has in the past, is evolving its business model, focusing more on software—the fastest growing segment in the storage sector. EMC is, in

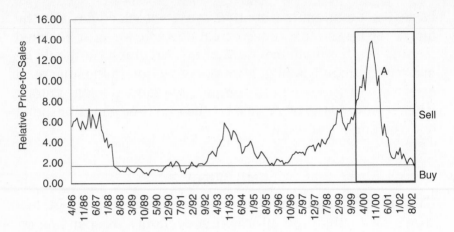

Figure 7.6   EMC (EMC) Relative Price-to-Sales Ratio
Source: Data from Compustat.

essence, once again staying one step ahead of the competition—a trait of industry leaders. (See Appendix C for a sample Twelve Factor Fundamental Analysis on EMC.)

EMC is another good example of how RPSR works. Purchasing the stock in December 1995, and selling it once it entered the sell range in December 1999 would yield a 2,742.3 percent return, compared to a 155.2 percent return on the S&P 500.

Home Depot (HD)

Home Depot (HD) is a fallen-angel growth company, as well as an industry leader with a history of strong growth and innovation in the home improvement segment. Founded in 1978, HD is the world's largest home improvement retailer, with over 1,400 stores in the United States, Canada, and Latin America. HD is known for providing shoppers with the lowest prices and the highest levels of customer service.

HD was trading at high multiples in the early 1990s primarily due to its growth stock status and investors' correspondingly high expectations for the stock. However, the company was

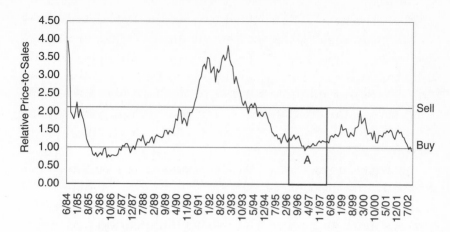

Figure 7.7 Home Depot (HD) Relative Price-to-Sales Ratio
Source: Data from Compustat.

pushed into the buy range in the mid-1990s (see Area A of Figure 7.7) due to a series of lawsuits related to sexual discrimination claims made by female employees, which resulted in the company paying out $65 million in an out-of-court settlement, and then another $1.7 million in a single lawsuit settled in 1997.

By late 1999, the stock was almost pushed into the sell range due to the booming consumer and real estate market, with the company delivering consistent earnings in excess of 22 percent.

An investor who purchased the stock in January 1997, and held on until September 30, 2002 (when the stock had not yet reached the sell line), would have experienced a 142.2 percent gain compared to the S&P 500 return for the same period of 12.4 percent.

Nike (NKE)

Nike (NKE) is the number one athletic shoe and apparel seller in the world, and is an interesting example of a company we liked at one time, but no longer hold (as we feel there are other more attractive opportunities at the moment).

From the late 1980s through most of the 1990s, NKE stock was outside the buy range and generally firmly in the sell range—an industry leading growth stock. Michael Jordan's affiliation with NKE in 1985 revolutionized the industry, as kids across the country wanted to be "just like Mike." The next wave of the company's growth was driven by the signing of professional golfer Tiger Woods as a company spokesperson.

As NKE moved into the late 1990s and early 2000s, it dropped into the buy range (see Figure 7.8). A number of factors were to blame, including the reduction of Michael Jordan's marketing power, increasing competition from other athletic shoe companies (notably Adidas), the rise of the "brown" shoe as casual day became a permanent fixture in corporate America, and the Asian flu in 1998 (Asia became an increasingly important market for NKE as athletic-oriented fashions went out of style elsewhere). See page 54 for additional information on the assessment of NKE from a "Franchise" perspective.

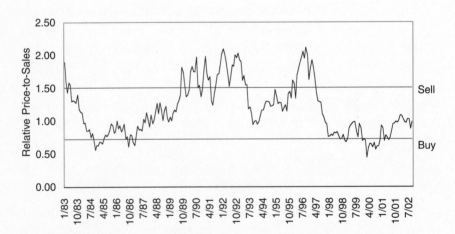

Figure 7.8   Nike Inc.—Class B (NKE) Relative Price-to-Sales Ratio
Source: Data from Compustat.

In the case of NKE, if an investor purchased shares in August of 1998, when the stock moved into the buy range and continued to hold until September 2002 (the stock has not reach reached the sell range), NKE would have returned 30.0% versus -10.1 for the S&P 500.

Cisco Systems (CSCO)

Cisco (CSCO) is the world's leading supplier of computer networking products and also a player in the telecommunications networking market. The company almost appeared in the buy range in June 1994 and did move into the buy range in April 1997 (the shaded areas of Figure 7.9). In both cases, weak end-demand and the fear of heightened competition hit the stock hard, and the stock price subsequently doubled as the company continued to outpace industry growth.

In the current downturn, expectations for growth in the company's core router business have come down to more realistic levels. However, CSCO is still the industry leader and is expected to continue to grow at a faster level than the

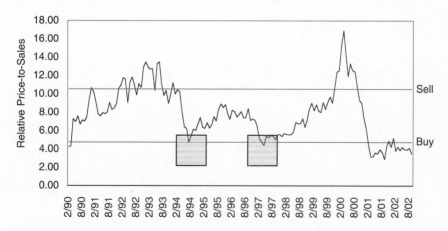

Figure 7.9 Cisco Systems Inc. (CSCO) Relative Price-to-Sales Ratio
Source: Data from Compustat.

industry. The company's valuation is also commensurate with the current level of expectations and its ability to develop and exploit new markets, which is stronger than ever.

Another good example of how RPSR works is the recent performance of CSCO stock. A gain of 734.0 percent versus 90.9 percent for the S&P 500 would have resulted from purchasing when CSCO entered the buy range in March 1997, and selling when it hit the sell range in November 1999.

THE INTERSECTION OF RDY AND RPSR

When looking at RDY and RPSR valuation methodologies, an investor is likely to ask whether stocks that were RPSR stocks can then become RDY stocks and, at that point, which is the better method for evaluating these stocks. The answer is that stocks evaluated with RPSR can occasionally become buyable with RDY. The overarching rule is that when RDY becomes applicable to RPSR stocks (e.g., the stock price declines enough that the dividend yield rises above the market yield), investors need to pay close attention and may be served better by switching to RDY as the valuation methodology. Additionally, it is interesting to note that in those cases, RDY may provide a more rigorous measure of value. We have found that when RDY signals a buy in stocks that we had previously measured using RPSR, it generally marks the bottom in relative price. The stocks that are most likely to fall into this category are growth companies that have moved through their growth phase into a state of maturation.

It is most valuable to look at this phenomenon in the context of some actual examples.

Limited Brands (LTD)

Limited (LTD) began in 1963 as a single store focused on affordable fashions for teenagers and young women. Today, LTD is a mature company that includes stores such as The

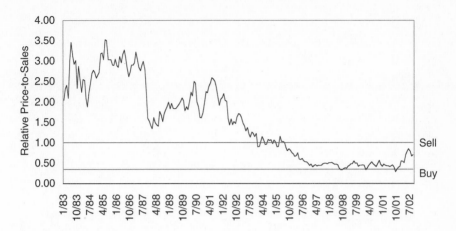

Figure 7.10 Limited Brands Inc. (LTD) Relative Price-to-Sales Ratio
Source: Data from Compustat.

Limited, Express, Lerner New York, Victoria's Secret, and Bath & Body Works. In recent years the company has refocused by closing stores and divesting itself of certain businesses, such as Lane Bryant.

When we first began investing in LTD, we looked at it from an RPSR perspective. As shown in Figure 7.10, the company first came into the RPSR buy range in August 1998 and has hovered in or near the buy range since then. If an investor purchased the stock August 30, 1998, and sold it on September 30, 2002 (when the stock had not yet reached the sell range), this investment would have returned 56.8 percent versus −10.1 percent for the S&P 500.

If LTD is viewed on an RDY basis a somewhat different picture emerges. Figure 7.11 shows the multiple opportunities to buy and sell since 1995, creating returns in excess of those available through the use of RPSR.

With RDY, the first buying opportunity was in March 1997, and a sell was then indicated in May 1999. This transaction would have resulted in a return of 181.7 percent for LTD versus 77.8 percent for the S&P 500.

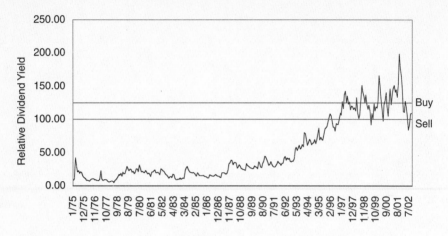

Figure 7.11 Limited Brands Inc. (LTD) Relative Dividend Yield
Source: Data from Compustat.

Again, in December 1999, the stock was in the buy range. A buy at that time and a subsequent sell in May 2000, based on RDY signals, would have generated an 11.8 percent gain versus −2.8 percent for the S&P 500.

With RDY there was one more opportunity to buy and sell LTD. A purchase of the stock in July 2000, and subsequent sale in June 2002, would have resulted in an 8.2 percent gain versus a 29.0 percent loss for the S&P 500. Usually an 8 percent gain over a two-year period would not be particularly desirable but, in a bear market a single digit gain is a victory.

In looking closer at the LTD RDY chart in Figure 7.12, one can see that the RDY buy signals coincide with the lowest levels of relative price (note the boxed areas).

LTD's RDY history provided valuable information, as well as more opportunities to buy and sell the stock based on changes in investor sentiment. We are fairly confident this stock will stay within ranges that favor evaluating it with RDY instead of RPSR.

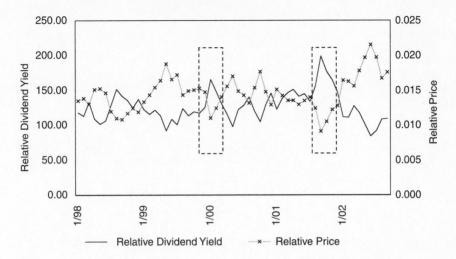

Figure 7.12   Limited Brands Inc. (LTD) Relative Dividend Yield and Relative Price
Source: Data from Compustat.

Hewlett-Packard (HPQ)

Hewlett-Packard (HPQ) recently made history with its Compaq acquisition. Not only was the acquisition large by any measure, it was one of the most controversial, as shareholder approval was marginal and the vote was highly publicized and lobbied.

In the late 1980s HPQ's growth began to slow somewhat, and the stock entered the RPSR buy range for the first time. By the mid-1990s, the stock had cycled in and out of the buy range a number of times, establishing a regular and reliable pattern. If an investor purchased it on July 31, 1998, after a buy was indicated, and later sold on July 30, 1999, at the end of the month when a sell was indicated, the returns would have been 90.4 percent for HPQ versus 20.2 percent for the S&P 500. (See Figure 7.13.)

Again, RPSR indicated a buy in November 2000. An investor who bought on that date and sold on September 30, 2002 (when there was still no signal to sell) would have realized a 61.9 percent loss on HPQ versus a −36.4 percent return for the S&P 500. This is not a terribly successful investment.

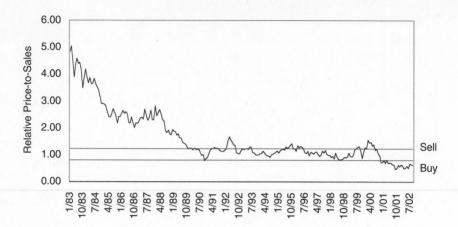

Figure 7.13   Hewlett-Packard Co. (HPQ) Relative Price-to-Sales Ratio
Source: Data from Compustat.

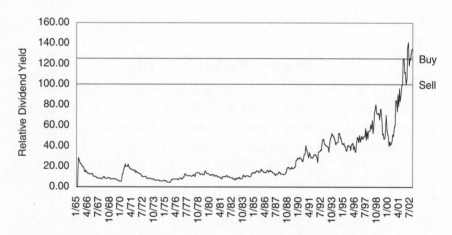

Figure 7.14   Hewlett-Packard Co. (HPQ) Relative Dividend Yield
Source: Data from Compustat.

However, it appears HPQ is motoring into a slow growth, higher-than-market yielding stock. RDY is now a more appropriate valuation metric, which would explain poor results with RPSR. If you look at HPQ from an RDY perspective, an investor would have bought in September 2001, and sold in January

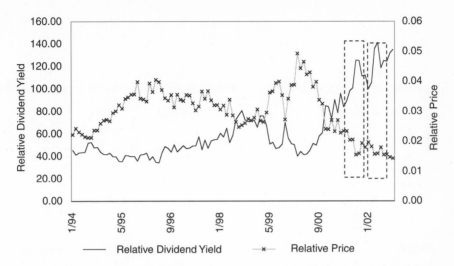

Figure 7.15 Hewlett-Packard Co. (HPQ) Relative Dividend Yield and Relative Price
Source: Data from Compustat.

2002. This approach (assuming month-end transaction dates) would have resulted in a 38.3 percent return on HPQ compared to 9.1 percent for the S&P 500. (See Figure 7.14.)

If an investor looks at a smaller section of the RDY chart, he or she can see that, like LTD, RDY buys are indicating lows in relative price for HPQ. This stock has transformed from a fallen-angel growth stock to a more traditional value holding. We believe RDY will identify the valuation turning points with great success. (Shown in boxed areas of Figure 7.15.)

Electronic Data Systems Corporation (EDS)

Electronic Data Systems Corporation (EDS), the largest independent computer management and services company in the United States, is another interesting example of the intersection of RPSR and RDY. The company has had an interesting history. It was founded by Ross Perot, later sold to General Motors (GM issued a tracking stock for EDS), and subsequently spun off from GM.

Figure 7.16 Electronic Data Systems Corp. (EDS) Relative Price-to-Sales Ratio
Source: Data from Compustat.

The company has been buyable on an RPSR basis since May 1998, and has not yet entered the sell range as of the time of publication. If an investor would have bought the stock May 29, 1998, and held onto the stock through September 30, 2002, the return would have been −59.7 percent versus −20.8 percent for the S&P 500. (See Figure 7.16.)

Again, RDY provides another perspective on EDS, signaling a buy in June 2000, and a subsequent sell in November 2000. Assuming month-end transactions, this would have resulted in a more favorable 29.1 percent gain versus −9.2 percent for the S&P 500. (See Figure 7.17.)

Again, when looking at a shorter section of the RDY chart plotted with relative price, one can see that RDY is marking lows in the relative price of EDS. (See the box in Figure 7.18.)

It is interesting to note that EDS was originally purchased as an RPSR stock and then held onto. During this time the company announced a significant earnings shortfall in mid-2002 causing its share price to collapse. Though the dividend yield quickly rose to more than 4 percent, our discipline also required us to re-evaluate the Twelve Fundamental Factors. In the end, we ended up failing the company on several factors

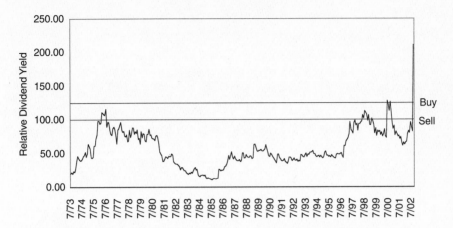

Figure 7.17 Electronic Data Systems Corp. (EDS) Relative Dividend Yield
Source: Data from Compustat.

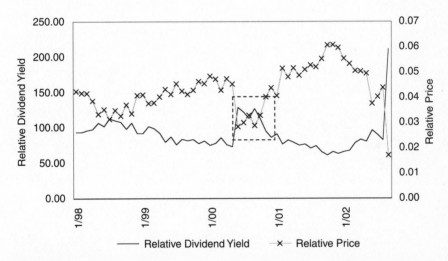

Figure 7.18 Electronic Data Systems Corp. (EDS) Relative Dividend Yield and
Relative Price
Source: Data from Compustat.

(management, cash flow, and financial risk), exiting our position, and avoiding the mistake of staying with a newly created
value-trap. This stresses the fact that both the RDY and
RPSR valuation methodologies must always be coupled with

the Twelve Fundamental Factors and at times reassessment may result in a company failing the evaluation criteria.

The transformation of former fallen-angel growth stocks bought and sold using RPSR into traditional value stocks more appropriately valued using RDY does not negate the value of one discipline over another. It does urge, however, for the application of the *right* discipline for a given group of stocks.

8

CONSTRUCTING A VALUE-DRIVEN PORTFOLIO

Investors . . . "should take extreme care to own not the most, but the best. In a field of common stocks, a little bit of a great many can never be more than a poor substitute for a few of the outstanding."

Phillip Fisher

Building a value-driven portfolio using RDY and RPSR is not significantly different from building portfolios in general. Our portfolio construction guidelines are driven by the desire to build a portfolio of the highest quality, most attractively valued companies. In addition, we want to selectively diversify a portfolio to minimize longer-term volatility and outperform the market over the long term. Essentially, the RDY and RPSR methodologies drive us into taking a growth-at-a-reasonable-price approach to investing.

The portfolio construction process starts with a pool of stocks that have met either the RDY or RPSR criteria, as well as the Twelve Fundamental Factors analysis tests. As you will see, if a stock passes the RDY/RPSR screen and the Twelve Fundamental Factors, it does not automatically mean that one should buy the stock. At any given time we might have a pool of fifty or sixty stocks that meet our criteria, and we keep an eye on all of them. But we will only assemble a portfolio out of those we feel have the best current potential to generate above-market returns over the long term. This can only be achieved by creating a disciplined, systematic approach to portfolio construction that is dedicated to optimizing potential return while managing risk.

To realize this goal, five key proprietary factors have been identified over the years:

1. Concentration

2. Selecting only the "best" companies

3. Use of both RDY and RPSR stocks

4. Covariance

5. Weightings/Diversification

1. **Concentration**. The first principle of concentration is especially significant. It's best to limit oneself to between twenty-five and thirty-five stocks. Peter Bernstein, the founder of the *Journal of Portfolio Management*, wrote, "Diversification is the only rational deployment of our ignorance." Every portfolio manager who has tried to hedge his or her bets by adding more stocks to a portfolio knows the truth of this statement. There is a substantial body of research that shows that a portfolio containing under twenty stocks is optimal in terms of diversification. Additional holdings do not reduce portfolio standard deviation in any meaningful way. More specifically, very small portfolios result in an increase in the level of volatility without significantly increasing return, while a larger portfolio begins to take on index-like characteristics without significantly increasing return.[1] Other research shows that, for mutual funds, a portfolio of ten to twenty stocks is most desirable. Figure 8.1 illustrates this point.

In our mind, though, a portfolio of ten to twenty stocks is decidedly impractical. In the institutional

Mutual Funds

Stocks Owned	10-20	21-30	31-40	41-50	51-70	71-100	101+
Number of Firms	14	82	129	166	273	270	431
Average 10 Year Return	13.76%	9.39%	10.21%	10.33%	11.02%	10.98%	10.91%
S&P 500 10 Year Return	12.08%	12.08%	12.08%	12.08%	12.08%	12.08%	12.08%
Excess Return	1.68%	-2.69%	-1.87%	-1.75%	-1.06%	-1.10%	-1.17%

Figure 8.1 Impact of Diversification on Returns Large Cap Funds
Source: Data from Morningstar Principia Pro (5/30/02).

world, clients and prospects alike are often averse to having a great deal of money invested in a very small number of stocks. Additionally, in a highly volatile market, such as that seen in the first half of 2002, the portfolio would be subject to excessively sharp swings in the short term. With our investment approach, a portfolio of twenty-five to thirty-five stocks results in an optimal blend to maximize performance without overdiversifying, while maintaining reasonable levels of risk.

Concentrating the portfolio in twenty-five to thirty-five stocks confers another important advantage. Table 8.1 illustrates a problem faced by every large cap portfolio manager—given the size of the large cap universe, one must either concentrate the portfolio or invest in a relatively limited universe of stocks. For a 100-stock large cap portfolio, investors are limited to selecting 1 out of every 2.8 stocks. When investors concentrate the portfolio in thirty stocks, the selection ratio becomes a much more favorable 1 out of 9.

Table 8.1 Problems faced by Large Cap Portfolio Managers

	Market Cap	Number of Companies	Opportunity Ratio
Large Cap	Over $10 billion	276	1 in 2.8
Mid Cap	$3–$10 billion	422	1 in 4.2
Small Cap	Under $3 billion	8,637	1 in 86.4

Source: Compustat, September 2002.

From a portfolio management perspective, concentrating a portfolio has other advantages as well. Every management firm finds that analysts' time is a scarce commodity that needs to be allocated carefully. A tremendous amount of research to screen candidate stocks is needed, followed by ongoing analytics to ensure that the stock continues to perform as expected. Concentrating analytical firepower on a smaller number of stocks increases one's ability to pick stocks with strong upside potential. Conversely, the portfolio manager can move faster and more intelligently when a holding begins to underperform, and either reduce or add to the position as conditions warrant. Holding fewer names also allows investors to better manage the overall relationship between the various stocks in the portfolio.

2. **Selecting only the "best" companies**. This second principle may seem self-evident, but in actual practice is rarely achieved. In the investing industry, it is not uncommon to see a manager with fifty stocks—including perhaps twenty great stocks and thirty other stocks that are not so great, but that are required in order to meet the portfolio's guidelines. The "only invest in the best" rule is particularly important when investing in fallen-angel growth stocks, which require a high degree of selectivity via fundamental research.

3. **Use of both RDY and RPSR stocks**. A portfolio that combines RDY and RPSR stocks offers several advantages: The RPSR stocks allow us to find situations where a return to a former growth curve, even at a more modest rate of climb, will fuel a company's share price: providing a capital gains kicker. The RDY stocks provide the added leverage that dividends give to the portfolio, as well as exposure to some of the less-volatile sectors of the market. RDY is the tortoise to RPSR's hare.

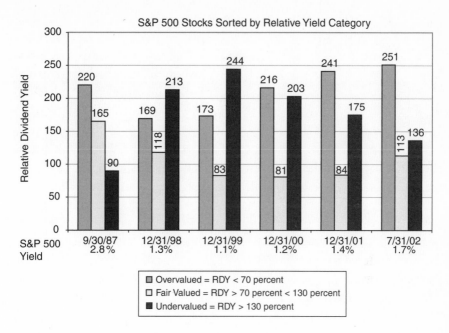

Figure 8.2 Distribution of Relative Yield Levels
Source: Data from Compustat.

Figure 8.2 is an interesting illustration of why a combination of RDY and RPSR stocks is appropriate—over time, there is a shifting ratio of companies buyable through RDY. RPSR always enables investors to have a large enough universe from which to select stocks.

4. **Covariance**. The fourth principle is managing covariance of return whenever possible, with covariance being a measure of correlation between various industries and sectors. Over time certain industry groups and/or sectors tend to exhibit a strong negative covariance with each other: when one group is generating excess return, the other is underperforming. By considering covariance in the portfolio construction process, investors have the opportunity to reduce the overall volatility of the portfolio.

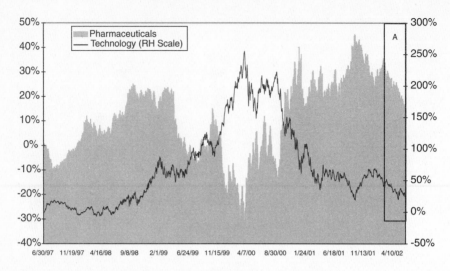

Figure 8.3 Percentage Change in Price Relative to the S&P: Technology versus Pharmaceutical Stocks June 1997–June 2002
Source: Data from Fact Set.

Look, for example, at Figure 8.3. This chart depicts the relationship between drug stocks and technology stocks. For a long period of time, they have been almost mirror images of each other in terms of relative performance. When technology stocks are up, pharmaceuticals are down, and vice versa. This is because technology stocks tend to outperform when earnings growth is robust and pharmaceuticals tend to outperform when overall earnings growth slows and their steady, relative earnings growth becomes more attractive. This inverse relationship between technology and pharmaceutical companies has generally held until 2002, when both technology and pharmaceutical stocks have declined, presenting a challenge to portfolio managers (see Area A of Figure 8.3). At the time of writing it is impossible to tell whether this is a secular change or a cyclical aberration. Investors should continue to monitor these two industries because negative covariance

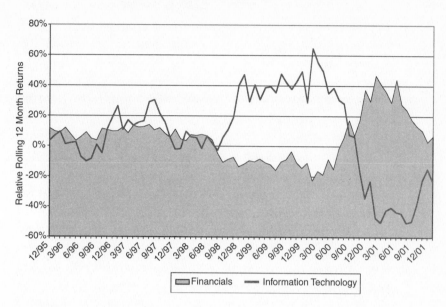

Figure 8.4 Information Technologies and Financials Rolling Twelve-Month Returns Relative to the S&P 500
Source: Data from Bloomberg.

between them can be a powerful portfolio management tool if it reasserts itself.

A similar inverse relationship currently exists between information technology and financial companies. As Figure 8.4 illustrates, these industries have exhibited a strong negative correlation since the late 1990s.

We observed this relationship and have incorporated it into our portfolio management discipline, increasing our commitment to the financial sector as an offset to our technology holdings. By testing various models, investors may find that this is yet another means of controlling portfolio volatility while keeping their focus on investing in only the "best" companies.

5. **Weightings/Diversification**. The fifth principle is related to the weighting of both sectors and individual holdings. In terms of sector weightings, we will not, as

a rule, allow a sector to reach more than twice the S&P sector weighting. Rarely, we may also choose to deliberately overweight a sector if we believe that the general economic conditions warrant. At the time of this writing, our portfolios are overweight in the beaten-down technology sector and underweight in the consumer nondurables group as we have trimmed back or sold stocks into the strong performance of the sector in 2002.

Individual securities are purchased in stages. When we first initiate a holding we will generally buy a position of up to 0.5 percent of the overall portfolio. We will then continue to accumulate shares over time to reach a total weighting of approximately 3 to 5 percent. When buying any stock, we don't believe we can accurately predict the exact bottom in the price, so we take an "average-in" approach. In viewing the charts, the patterns support this approach, as stocks can get cheaper after entering the buy range. The same holds true on the sell side. Value investors should be mentally prepared for this. It provides an opportunity for averaging in and averaging out. We do not generally allow any given stock to grow to more than 6 percent of the value of the entire portfolio. *This is an important component of the development of the portfolio.* Since we are purchasing value stocks, we are buying them when they are cheap, making it relatively easy to accumulate a large holding of a given stock over time and still not exceed our percentage rule. But what happens once the stock begins to rise? First we trim the position as appropriate to ensure that it does not exceed a 6 percent portfolio weighting. Second, once the stock hits the sell line, we will begin to sell the position with the objective of exiting before the stock moves out of the sell range through price decline. Maintaining the relative weighting in the portfolio allows investors to keep their investing risk at an acceptable level, which is particularly important in today's fast-moving and volatile markets.

When we initially buy a stock, we plan to hold it for a long period of time, typically one to three years. However, we continually evaluate our current holdings against the universe of stocks meeting the RDY/RPSR and Twelve Fundamental Factors screens. If a candidate stock is offering more promise than an existing holding, we will begin to rotate that stock into the portfolio, while we rotate out the less-attractive holding. These decisions are all based on what the stock looks like in terms of RDY or RPSR and what the Twelve Fundamental Factors analysis has revealed about each stock. In difficult market periods, portfolio managers often have the opportunity to "upgrade" their portfolio as the market sell-off inevitably affects even the highest quality stocks.

Often, when we add a stock to our portfolio, we know that there is a potential for the stock to drop further. Once a pattern of bad news surrounds a company, Wall Street will continue to beat the "negative news" drums as holders of the stock head for the exits. The result? The stock loses its shareholder constituency. Generally these stocks are totally neglected and languish until a new constituency, usually value investors, begins to see an over punished stock as an attractive value and a new constituency is developed. As the news flow improves new buyers come in—a new constituency, if you will. Momentum works both ways and stocks often continue to move long after the news is priced into the stock. That will always be the good news for value investors.

A word about hedge funds: volatility has been exacerbated by the proliferation of hedge funds in recent years (the number has quadrupled over the past ten years). There are an increasing number of hedge fund managers ready to profit on short-term movements—short or

long—and their shorter-term transactional orientation
has added materially to market and specific stock
volatility. Although the marked increase in volatility in
recent years can be a distraction, it also consistently creates the opportunity to buy some very high-quality companies at extremely attractive valuations.

But what happens if a stock starts to look less and less
like an attractive investment and it cannot find a floor?
When we originally began investing using RDY, we did
not often see stocks decline further than 50 percent
after entering the buy range. The very nature of RDY led
us to stocks that were already discounting bad news. As
we expanded our discipline to RPSR, we were focused
on a group of stocks that were inherently more volatile
than the RDY stocks. The *potential* for wider swings on
the up- and downside existed, and we needed to learn to
manage the higher level of risk associated with investing
in these stocks.

Figure 8.5 shows the unusually high level of volatility
prevalent in the market since approximately January
2000. It's obvious that the number of stocks underperforming the Russell 1000 Index by 30 percent or more
has skyrocketed during this period—well above the
norm since 1979. According to Morgan Stanley, the
odds of a stock underperforming the Index by 30
percent or more in a given month during this period
have been six times higher than the historical average.
That is a stunning increase and should put into
perspective the poor performance many mutual funds
have experienced since January 2000. There have been
very few places to hide in this market rout, particularly
for managers with relatively concentrated holdings.
Look again at the chart—it is remarkable! Of course we
have been suffering through the worst bear market
since the Great Depression, which means stocks are
generally declining, but the magnitude and velocity is

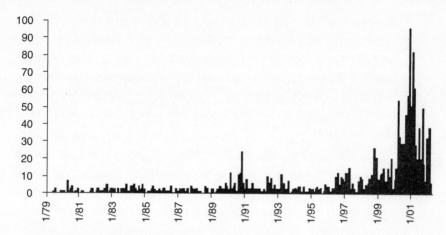

Figure 8.5   30 percent + Relative Underperformers
Source: Data from Morgan Stanley Research.

what is notable. To adapt to this new reality, we have adopted a new portfolio rule—stop-loss orders. Today the discipline encompasses two separate triggers to address both short- and long-term declines. The two triggers, along with some insight into why the triggers were set where they were and what actions should be taken after a trigger point is hit, follow. Trigger #1 is the key driver:

Trigger #1: A relative price decline of 10 percent in one day or 15 percent in two days causes an automatic trim to one-half of the pre-decline position size (e.g., a 4 percent position would get cut to 2 percent).

Why 10 percent? A 10 percent move in one day probably indicates that an unanticipated stock-specific event has occurred.

Why automatic? An automatic sell avoids holding a stock that continues to drift on negative sentiment and selling as the street digests the news.

What's next? The new information, including likely near-term sentiment, is evaluated and the original investment thesis is reassessed. We will take one of two clear-cut courses of action: We will either (1) sell out of the position altogether, or (2) add to the position at a specified level, after we identify the new "absolute rock bottom valuation aggressive add level," and the "specific catalysts" that will move the stock higher.

Trigger #2: A price decline of 20 percent in the past week or over one, three, six, or twelve months causes (1) a quick Twelve Fundamental Factors reassessment of the company, while (2) an incremental 5 percent decline causes an automatic trim to one-half the pre-decline position size.

Why have this second trigger? A downward revaluation of this magnitude indicates that our thesis and fundamental work may have failed (the stock is clearly not working as planned) or that something material has changed investor sentiment. We may have invested in the stock too early, we may have misjudged where true valuation support would be found, or we may have been wrong about the catalysts that we thought would boost the stock. Whatever the cause, we must be able to admit when an investment idea is not working, and act quickly.

Why multiple periods? The objective is to identify stocks that "dribble-off" due to a gradual shift in sentiment. Having multiple review periods avoids statistical anomalies, such as a 9 percent decline that occurs over three successive months or quarters.

Why not automatic? When viewing price movements over a longer time frame, relative performance must first be considered.

What's next? We must perform a quick Twelve Fundamental Factors analysis and recommend that we either (1) sell out of the position, or (2) add to the position at a specified level, after the new "absolute rock bottom valuation/aggressive add level" and the "specific catalysts" that will move the stock higher are identified.

Before leaving the portfolio management process, it is also important to look at some of the "learning experiences"—also known as MISTAKES! As part of the ongoing portfolio management process, we have learned, generally the hard way, that there are certain types of stocks that we should not buy, no matter how attractive they look based on our own criteria.

MERGED COMPANIES COMBINING HIGH-GROWTH AND SLOW-GROWTH COMPONENTS

Often these are the result of mergers of high-growth companies with old-line, dividend-paying firms, such as the merger of telephone company US West with a high-flying fiber-optic cable company to form Qwest, or the merger of media behemoth Time Warner with Internet powerhouse AOL. Both resultant companies combine high-growth components with low-growth businesses and have been saddled with massive amounts of debt that must be whittled off the books before the "real" future company can emerge. In early 2002, AOL Time Warner took a $54 billion write-down on Goodwill relating to assets that were combined during the merger, the largest such write-down of value in corporate history. It is hard to imagine exactly how, under the circumstances, it is possible to gauge relative value, since it is impossible to know from whence future growth will emerge. For example, as of this writing, contrary to all expectations at the time of the merger, most of the growth in AOL Time Warner has come from the old Time Warner. (It is interesting to note that at the time the AOL Time Warner merger was announced, AOL was trading at $73 per share. However, as of June 30, 2002, the merged company was trading at $15 per share.) What makes these companies dangerous for RDY and RPSR investors is that historical RDY and/or RPSR data is no longer relevant, since the previous history is based on a different earnings growth rate and the combined companies have no operating experience. We made this mistake with Qwest, which has gone down as one of the worst investments we have made in our portfolios and the inspiration for our stop-loss rule.

NEW COMPANIES WITH TOO SHORT A HISTORY

Lucent is probably the best example of a company whose operating history as a public company is at the time of this writing still too short to make sound judgments. Although the roots of Lucent go all the way back to 1856, even before the telephone was invented, Lucent—which spent most of its life as the Western Electric division (later Bell Labs) of telephone giant AT&T—did not actually come into existence as an independent company until 1996. The thinking at the time was that spinning out Western Electric to shareholders would create increased value because, as a division of AT&T, its sales growth was impeded by telecom companies that did not want to purchase equipment from a competitor. For a while, the spinout strategy worked. Lucent quickly became the market leader in telecommunications gear, more than doubling its sales between 1996 and 1999. Moreover, earnings were growing at an even more rapid rate, fifteen-fold in the same period, while its stock price rose only eight-fold. From both a price-to-sales perspective and an EPS perspective, Lucent looked like an obvious winner, and the RPSR methodology showed it to be a clear buy. But Lucent had entered the market in the midst of the largest telecommunications boom in history, fueled by Internet growth. When that cooled off, Lucent's sales began to fall, exacerbated by a new product and research miscalculation by management which gave the advantage to the competition in the latest product cycle. Without a long operating history, the buy and sell ranges using RPSR were not statistically meaningful, which should have been recognized. In this case RPSR was a dismal failure and the Twelve Fundamental Factor analysis was not terribly helpful.

> *Note:* Lucent is different from Estee Lauder, which we also bought with less than ten years of history. In this case, Estee Lauder was an established company that later went public in the same form and with the same management, generating confidence when paired with an RPSR chart with a relatively consistent pattern.

Taken together, everything that we are doing in the way of portfolio construction and management is meant to provide investors with a measured approach to creating wealth with a value-oriented method. We attempt to take into account the sweeping changes that have taken place in the markets since the origination of value investing more than seventy years ago. By using portfolio construction as a tool to lower volatility, we set the stage for much more predictable returns relative to the market. The components of our portfolio that produce a dividend add to the total return and should dampen the volatility of returns over the long term. The fallen-angel growth stock components provides potential for strong capital gains. A portfolio constructed according to these principles should perform between the S&P Barra Growth and S&P Barra Value Indices. Given this approach, it is logical that this investment style might be most easily thought of as "growth at a reasonable price." But because it is based upon underlying relative value, the approach stands four-square in the midst of value methodology and discipline, a topic discussed further in Chapter 9.

NOTE

1. For further information see John L. Evans and Stephen H. Archer "Diversification and the Reduction of Dispersion: An Empirical Analysis," *The Journal of Finance*, Volume 23, Issue 5 (December 1968); and James T. Mao, "Essentials of Portfolio Diversification," *The Journal of Finance*, Volume 25, Issue 5 (December 1970).

9

WHAT IS VALUE INVESTING TODAY?

"Growth and value investing are joined at the hip."

Warren Buffett

It's not clear what the consensus definition of value investing is today. In the last several years, a proliferation of new stock market indices have appeared, placing stocks into growth or value categories based on price-to-book ratios. For example, large cap stocks whose P/B ratios are above the median of the S&P 500 are thrown into the S&P 500 Growth Index. Those with P/B below the median are placed in the S&P 500 Value Index. The same process is used in the relatively new mid- and small cap indices as well.

Leading mutual fund industry monitoring firms such as Morningstar and Lipper Analytical Services also put funds into growth and value categories across the market capitalization spectrum, based primarily on portfolio price/earnings and/or price/book ratios. Although this is an honest effort to help investors differentiate between growth- and value-oriented funds, the focus on select quantitative factors in isolation can be misleading.

This brings us back to value investing. Buying second-rate companies in slow-growth industries trading at justifiably low P/E ratios is not, in our opinion, value investing and certainly not a strategy likely to produce sustainably good long-term investment returns. We believe that buying the best companies at the most attractive valuations relative to their peers, the broad market, and their own valuation history—the cornerstone of our Relative Value Discipline which combines the use of RDY and RPSR—is a more legitimate and productive value-oriented strategy.

The RDY and RPSR disciplines are designed to identify stocks with potentially strong fundamentals that, for whatever reason, are out-of-favor in the market or, worse yet, being shunned by investors. We believe these stocks have far greater upside potential than downside risk, and if this upside potential happens to be secured by a dividend, so much the better. We are not particularly concerned whether Morningstar or Lipper Analytical puts us in the growth or value category, because we believe our definition of value is much more realistic than the rather simplistic quantitative approach used in many categorization processes. In fairness, these firms cannot feasibly analyze funds with multiple or complex qualitative inputs. They monitor thousands of mutual funds and must rely on objective and easy-to-quantify factors to measure and categorize funds. Following a strategy like ours could result in the equivalent of the square peg being forced into a round hole.

Another reason we believe blanket categorizations of value or growth are misleading is that, at some point, most companies have been, or will be, both. For example, railroads were the penultimate growth stocks of the late nineteenth and early twentieth centuries. Then, as the industry matured, they became value stocks. Later, the railroads became cyclical stocks, with earnings tied directly to the growth of the economy. Also, defense was a great growth industry when the government was pouring billions into defense during World War II, the Korean War, the Cold War, and later, Vietnam. With the end of the Cold

War, the defense stocks that survived became value stocks. Since the events of September 11, 2001, defense stocks are again exhibiting growth-stock characteristics, but only time will tell if they have returned to growth-stock status or will merely cycle around one more time. An even timelier example is technology, which put the capital "G" on growth-stock investing during the "Roaring 90s." However, as tech spending plummeted over the last two years, some of the very best technology companies now qualify as legitimate value stocks. We are quite confident they will once again become growth stocks. That is why we continue to have a fair share of leading technology companies in our portfolios even though the sector has been badly battered in the past couple of years. The beauty of our RDY and RPSR disciplines is that they make room for stocks that migrate from growth to value and back again.

The most famous value investor of our time, Warren Buffett, appears aligned in his view of "value." Some of his most profitable investments have been growth companies purchased at P/E ratios that would have scared off investors focusing on absolute valuations. Perhaps the best example is Coca-Cola, a classic growth company and one of Buffett's largest and most successful investments. Figure 9.1, which charts Coke's RDY from 1962 through July 2002, is a near-perfect illustration of a growth stock periodically slipping into fallen-angel status, and the effectiveness of the RDY approach in identifying when growth stocks become true value-oriented opportunities.

As shown in Figure 9.1, Coke stock was selling at below market yields from the early 1960s through the mid-1970s. This was a growth stock and out of the reach of traditional value investors. By the late 1970s problems arose: the price of sugar skyrocketed and container prices, driven by energy costs, went through the roof, putting pressure on Coke's profit margin. At the same time, questions were being raised about the saturation of the soft drink market. From 1974 to 1982, Coke's stock was not attractive to growth investors due to slowing

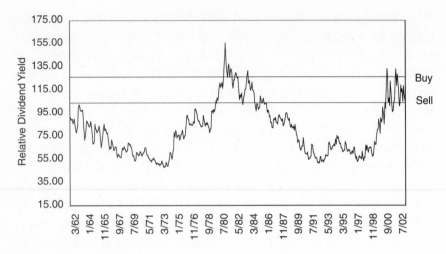

Figure 9.1   Coca-Cola Co. (KO) Relative Dividend Yield
Source: Data from Compustat.

earnings growth, nor was it yet attractive to value investors. The stock was suffering through a "classic" change in constituency. Coke's diversification into the entertainment business through Columbia Pictures and perceived lack of industry growth caused the company to retreat to its core businesses while the stock price languished. Under the leadership of CEO Robert Goizueta, Coke sold Columbia Pictures for a $1 billion profit and began a strong international expansion. During Goizueta's tenure, the market value of the company rose from $4 billion to $145 billion.

In 1997, Goizueta died of lung cancer, and his successor, Douglas Ivester, ran into a slew of problems that were directly related to Coke's rapid growth. In 1999, a deal to buy many of the beverage brands of Cadbury Schweppes had to be scaled down because of antitrust concerns. In the same year, Coke ran into a contamination problem at some of its European bottling plants, leading to an expensive product recall (a similar recall all but sank Perrier in the U.S. market), and then the European Commission charged the company with conspiring with competitors to fix market prices. By 2000, Ivester had resigned, and Coke came into value range again as the financial press and investors wrote off Coke as a growth stock. Since then, Coke has been a strong relative performer for value investors with a discipline.

Obviously, investing in Coke when it was trading at a low relative valuation would be a value investor's dream, because in addition to attractive valuations, the company has the ability to drive sustained and impressive earnings growth over time, and produce strong stock returns.

This same ability to identify valuation opportunities in growth stocks, which have fallen from favor, holds true for RPSR. Take a look at Amgen (AMGN). The RPSR chart in Figure 9.2 shows that the company came into the buy range in 1993 and again in 1997. With pharmaceutical and biotech companies, failed new product initiatives are often the catalyst to underperformance and opportunity for value investors. This was the case with AMGN. Specifically in 1997, the company reported the failure of drug trials for a treatment for Lou Gehrig's disease. This was followed by more bad news

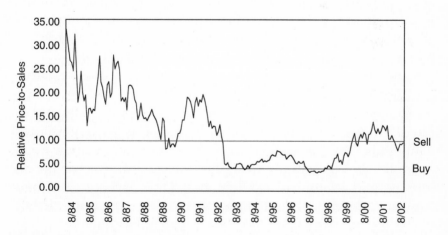

Figure 9.2 Amgen Inc. (AMGN) Relative Price-to-Sales Ratio
Source: Data from Compustat.

related to legal disputes with Johnson & Johnson. The stock moved into the sell range as its drug development process on new drugs progressed, and it successfully won several patent infringement lawsuits.

Most recently (in the last year), General Electric (GE) and Genentech (DNA), high-quality growth companies by any definition, fell into the value range. GE was recently trading at seventeen times earnings, an historically low P/E for such a high-quality growth stock. We focused on GE's strong and stable earnings history throughout economic cycles. GE is particularly attractive given its history of maintaining long-term double-digit earnings growth. So, from a value investor's perspective, buying GE at seventeen times earnings was a true value opportunity. Genentech is trading today at about the same price it was trading at three years ago, despite the fact that revenues have doubled. Even though it is trading at a premium to the market, biotechnology stocks as a whole (on a price-to-growth basis) are trading at prices that are cheaper than pharmaceuticals. Thus, Genentech, in terms of RPSR and other measures, still offers value relative to its own history and relative to other opportunities in the market. There are worries over some late stage drugs, but the pipeline is the most robust in the industry. Value investors learn to determine (as much as is humanly possible) when bad news is bad news and when bad news is already reflected in the price of the stock.

The moral of the story is that value is a truly relative proposition. At any given point, there are and will always be anomalies in the market—good companies with favorable long-term growth characteristics trading at attractive relative valuations. The question is whether an investment advisor can establish and maintain a discipline that allows him or her to identify and exploit these anomalies. The charts of Coke and Amgen, clearly demonstrate that the RDY and RPSR disciplines are well suited for this task. The results may not be visible every month or every quarter, but definitely are discernable over the long term. (See Appendix A.)

As stated earlier in the chapter, in my view, buying the best companies at the cheapest prices is the essence of value investing. When looking at stocks to invest in, it doesn't matter whether they are considered growth or value stocks by some accepted quantitative measures. The Relative Value Discipline helps develop a portfolio that, over the long term, has both growth and value characteristics, and allows investors to take advantage of opportunities usually out of the realm of the traditional value investor.

To determine the correct category for a Relative Value Discipline portfolio and its proper place in the asset allocation spectrum, one should examine the portfolio's characteristics. As illustrated in Figure 9.3, in a comparison of its fundamental characteristics versus the S&P Barra Growth and S&P Barra Value Indices, a portfolio following this strategy (using the Fremont New Era Value Fund offering as representative) would result in core-like exposure with a bias toward fallen-angel growth stocks.

	S&P Barra Value	Fremont New Era Value Fund*	S&P Barra Growth
Number of Holdings	336	32	164
Weighted Average Capitalization ($M)	$47,906	$71,923	$91,884
Yield	2.50%	1.74%	1.43%
Price/Book	1.95	3.63	5.94
Forecast P/E Ratio (FY1)	13.61	17.23	19.30
Est. Earnings Growth	11.77	13.21	14.78

*The Fremont New Era Value Fund is an open-ended mutual fund managed by a team at Fremont Investment Advisors including the author which follows the investing discipline outlined in this book. It provides a good representation of a portfolio constructed using Relative Value Discipline.

Figure 9.3   Fremont New Era Value Fund Portfolio Characteristics (as of September 30, 2002)
Source: Data from Fremont Investment Advisors.

10

SEVEN CRITICAL LESSONS WE HAVE LEARNED AS DISCIPLINED INVESTMENT MANAGERS

"Don't gamble; take all your savings and buy some good stock and hold it till it goes up, then sell it. If it don't go up, don't buy it."

Will Rogers

Part of the reason for creating the RDY and RPSR disciplines is that, over our collective years in the money management business, we have learned a number of useful lessons about investor behavior. Most of the lessons have emerged during periods of market uncertainty. After all, part of the reason for developing a discipline is to take human emotion out of the investing equation, which is most important during market extremes (on the upside and the downside). People tend to stay too long with stocks they like, or fail to go back to a stock that has been beaten down, even after there is a sustained period of good news. The following seven maxims are meant to show investors exactly why they should choose and stick with a time-tested investment discipline.

1. WALL STREET TENDS TO TAKE CURRENT TRENDS AND EXTRAPOLATE THEM OUT TO INFINITY.

"If you are going bankrupt, be sure you bankrupt on a big scale."

—Paul A. Samuelson

In the mid-to-late 1970s, when the U.S. economy was mired in a prolonged recession and stocks languished, it seemed to many that the country would never have prosperity again. In the 1990s, when the so-called "new economy" was exploding and the stock market was roaring, the rallying cry was that recessions and bear markets were a thing of the past. Both times, analysts, economists, media pundits, and investors alike were guilty of straight-line extrapolation, and both times, they were wrong. I believe this behavior was primarily driven by two factors:

▎ It is human nature to think things will continue as they are at any point in time. The herd mentality tends to have people crying "the sky is the limit" or screaming "the sky is falling."
▎ Wall Street analysts are measured on their ability to be accurate over the short term. This causes them to focus on the most recent data, and assume that today's trends will continue indefinitely. This short-term focus makes it impossible for them to spot market turning points. Discipline, therefore, is critical.

2. IT IS RARELY "DIFFERENT THIS TIME."

"Business will be better or worse."

—Calvin Coolidge

In this world of accelerated change, it seems that the more things change, the more they stay the same. One of the biggest challenges investors face is to resist believing the popular assumption that in any given situation "it is different this time." We saw this in the late 1990s as earnings became a non-issue in the valuation of companies. At the time we did not jump on the bandwagon of buying the high-flying Internet stocks, but we occasionally questioned ourselves. Of course, those stocks have declined precipitously from their peaks, and we have our investment discipline to thank for keeping us on the sideline.

Over time, however, certain businesses *do* change significantly and investors have to be prepared to understand and respond to these changes. The utilities industry is a good example. Deregulation in the 1990s dramatically altered the nature of the utilities industry. What was once a safe, secure, guaranteed rate-of-return business became a competitive free-for-all. In 1994, while buying utilities using the RDY discipline, the discipline began failing to identify periods of over- and undervaluation. RDY was not working because, in the increasingly competitive environment, utilities companies were raising or cutting their dividends without regard to underlying earnings. The typical negative correlation of RDY versus relative price was not holding (see Chapter 3). In response we sold all of our utility holdings. Then, in 1999 and 2000, the utilities appeared to get cheap again. We considered buying again—thinking maybe things were changing—but not enough data was available and we therefore took no action. Secular change does occur from time to time, but not as often as investors assume. It *did* occur with electric utilities, however. Below is a discussion of a group that was accused of secular change but was merely experiencing a cyclical downturn.

In the early 1990s, the market decided that banks were no longer attractive stocks and valuations declined significantly. The market's rationale was that banks were in a commodity business—the buying and selling of money—and that in a low interest rate environment, they could not hope to grow earnings without offering other services. Thus, the era of the "financial supermarket" was born. Citigroup, for example, acquired insurance companies, sub-prime (high interest) credit card firms, and brokerage houses, and at the same time began emphasizing international lending, all in an effort to boost the value of the company. In the recent economic downturn, however, all of these higher earning assets became liabilities, and those banks still tied directly to traditional spread businesses (mortgage and commercial lending) outperformed the financial supermarkets.

The most recent and dramatic illustration of "it is rarely different this time" was Internet stock valuations in the late 1990s. As dotcom valuations soared to mind-boggling highs, the market assumed that it was different this time. We saw the dotcoms simply as retailers with a new distribution channel—similar to traditional retailers with catalog businesses. We asked ourselves why these companies should have such lofty valuations. In hindsight we now know it wasn't different this time, and those stocks that soared into the stratosphere fell to earth with a loud thud.

Change can take place over time; for example, witness the electric utilities (previously discussed). Generally, though, the sentiment that "it is different this time" creates a buy or sell opportunity for the disciplined, astute investor.

3. MARKET WORKOUTS ARE OFTEN GREAT INVESTMENT OPPORTUNITIES.

"Listening to the economics wizards talk about the recession, you can get the feeling that things are going to get better as soon as they get worse."

—Russell Baker

Beginning with a technology-led market decline and followed by a general slowdown of the economy exacerbated by the events of September 11, 2001, the markets are in a workout phase.

Different industry groups are also subject to workouts. There have been many examples of workout opportunities over the years, but a good example of this phenomenon would be pharmaceutical stocks during the early 1990s, following Hillary Clinton's failed attempt at managed care reform. At that time, with potential government regulation looming, the pharmaceutical stocks took a valuation dive. The health care debate centered on cost containment, with high-priced drugs considered by some the major contributors to the explosion in health costs. As a result, drug stocks languished, and an era of consolidation in the industry began with a wave of mergers. However, when health care industry analysts did some real research, they found that drug therapies were often cheaper than the alternatives, such as surgical procedures. The push to centralized health care failed, and investors focused again on the underlying fundamentals. A newly consolidated drug industry rebounded, providing renewed investment opportunities. These are the times when value investors are challenged to keep the faith and are often rewarded with outstanding returns as the market goes back to a more normal state of affairs—remember, it is rarely "different this time."

4. AT TURNING POINTS, GO WITH YOUR DISCIPLINE —NOT WALL STREET.

"A man who knows the price of everything and the value of nothing" is the definition of a cynic.

—Oscar Wilde

As investment managers, we have never particularly trusted the buy and sell recommendations of Wall Street analysts. We do, however, find value in the factual research produced by Wall Street. It is difficult to match their depth of coverage and expertise when it comes to the facts.

Recall in earlier chapters the discussion about "constituencies." Meet the constituency makers. Value investors are typically buying stocks when there is a dearth of buy recommendations. Once the stock turns and begins to generate excess return, they often see Wall Street experience a change of heart. The second wave of outperformance is often generated by a spate of upgrades and a return of the growth stock "constituents" who cleared out when the company stumbled: "All value investors! Exit stage left."

It is that short-term focus that contributes to Wall Street's lackluster record at calling turning points for stocks. How many times have you watched the "penguins" march out on CNBC's *Squawk Box* and seen Wall Street analysts en masse downgrade a stock *after* the bad news? It's hard to understand how to make money selling a stock after it has declined. Moreover, it is not much better buying a stock after it has soared to new heights.

Analyst credibility and potential conflicts will be discussed in the following paragraphs. This is certainly not new news; however, years of experience working with Wall Street has taught us to value analysts' factual research and leave the buy and sell recommendations alone.

The credibility of analysts has recently come into question. Eliot Spitzer, the Attorney General for New York, investigated and exposed the impact of brokerage firms' profitable investment banking relationships on stock research (several analysts were found to have been touting investment banking client stocks while panning them in inter-office memos). The WorldCom debacle also focused attention on telecom analyst Jack Grubman, who was very close to WorldCom management, and maintained a strong buy on the stock until just prior to breaking news on the company's accounting scandal and its descent into bankruptcy. The byproduct is that all of this publicity (and the fact that brokerage firms will probably have to spend a big pile of money settling lawsuits from former clients) may lead to meaningful reform on Wall Street.

Figures 10.1 through 10.3 show the price action of Cisco Systems, Oracle, and Intel stocks, along with consensus Wall Street recommendations to illustrate just how untimely some analyst recommendations can be. You will note that the most bullish consensus on these stocks was very near stock price peaks and was followed by sharp declines.

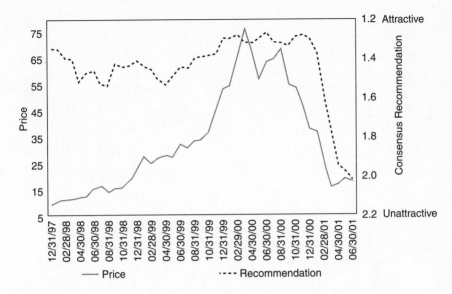

Figure 10.1 Price versus Recommendation, Cisco Systems, 07/18/01
Source: Data from I.B.E.S.

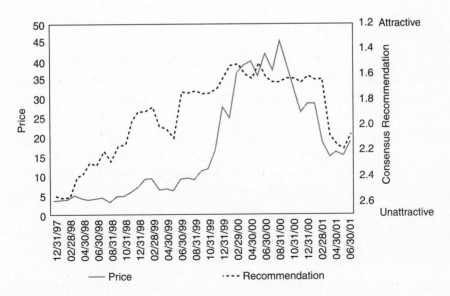

Figure 10.2 Price versus Recommendation, Oracle Corp., 07/18/01
Source: Data from I.B.E.S.

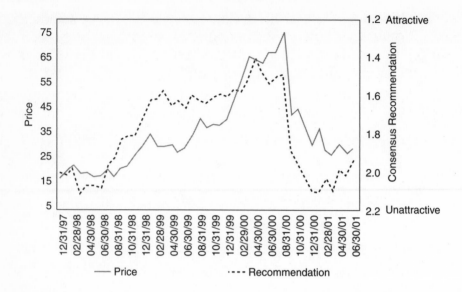

Figure 10.3   Price versus Recommendation, Intel Corp., 07/18/01
Source: Data from I.B.E.S.

Wall Street has taken quite a beating in recent years. Mentioning this fact is not intended to "pile on" additional abuse, which is best left to the media and the regulators. However, the upgrade/downgrade process has been particularly exasperating. The same people who were upgrading stocks while ignoring historical valuations in the late 1990s as the market and individual stocks traded at stratospheric multiples, are now downgrading stocks over two years into a bear market (again ignoring historical valuations).

The "upgrade/downgrade-after-the-fact" condition is not unique to Wall Street analysts. Economists also have rather dismal records in spotting economic and market turns. A recent article in *The Wall Street Journal* said "Economists from the Federal Reserve Bank of Atlanta recently studied the past 16 years of *The Wall Street Journal's* forecasting survey and found that economic prognosticators are at their worst when the economy is at a turning point, just when some sound advice on the outlook is most useful."[1]

5. INVESTMENT MANAGERS NEED TO CHALLENGE THEIR BELIEFS EVERY DAY.

". . . Work, work, work is the main thing."
—Abraham Lincoln

We humans are comfortable with what we know and are familiar with. Nevertheless, as an investor I would argue that we should be *more* uncomfortable with what we don't know and constantly seek to challenge what we *do* know. Feeling uncomfortable is *good*—because it makes us dig for the facts, which makes us better investors.

I will always be more comfortable buying a stock with great long-term fundamentals at a lower price rather than a higher price—as most investors would. Yet the method of determining the value of a stock and how to analyze the fundamentals is and should be constantly evolving.

Do not be afraid to take gains or limit your losses. Different market environments require different actions. In the late 1990s' bull market, selling stocks too soon was costly because they could double or triple again. Conversely, in the current bear market, complacency on the downside has been costly as well. Just as "letting-it-run" was the right pace for the bull market, "cutting-your-losses" has made sense in the bear market. (See the discussion of the stop-loss rule in Chapter 8.)

Adapting to the market does not mean an investor is undisciplined. Adapting within the framework of a discipline is the key.

6. USE THE AVAILABILITY OF DATA AND THE ALWAYS-ON FINANCIAL MEDIA TO YOUR ADVANTAGE.

"Do what you can, with what you have, where you are."
—Theodore Roosevelt

Over the last decade the press has served as a key source of timely information to investors. With the advent of CNBC, average investors have been given access to information that previously was limited to investment professionals. The improvement in the availability and quality of information is enormous, but also potentially dangerous for value investors.

Recall that when we are buying stocks the news is often bad. Given the format of most financial news shows, bad news can be repeated at a great frequency for extended periods, potentially pressuring stock prices further. What seemed like a "great value opportunity" can feel like a huge mistake. Avoid the temptation to become too focused on market commentary. If you are following a proven valuation discipline, have completed your fundamental analysis, and nothing has changed materially at the company, satisfy yourself once more, assuming that the bad news is already reflected in the price of the stock, and "hold on . . ." or buy more!

7. IT'S ALL RELATIVE.

"In principle there are no value judgments in economics."
—Milton Friedman

Value judgments may not have a place in economics, but investors are focused on the concept of value, and often don't agree on how to measure it.

When value-investing pioneers Benjamin Graham and David Dodd first began formulating their value-investing approach, they focused on an absolute measure of a company's valuation. I have always favored a relative approach to investing based on the theory that at times absolutes can provide the wrong answer or prevent an investor from taking advantage of true value-oriented opportunities. For instance, on an absolute valuation basis, companies such as Coke, General Electric, and Oracle almost always look too pricey for value investors. However, when one compares current valuations to their own histories and sectors, they have at times presented investors with significant opportunities. Warren Buffett's recent foray into buying fallen-angel technology stocks again verifies how the master of value investing is also focused on relative valuations.

NOTE

1. *The Wall Street Journal* (7/1/02).

APPENDIX A:
NEW ERA VALUE COMPOSITE

As an illustration of the investment discipline in action, consider the following composite performance for the New Era Value composite which uses the Relative Value Discipline approach to investing. Performance figures are as of September 30, 2002.

DISCLOSURE

The New Era Value composite is focused on a universe of undervalued securities which include traditional value securities and out-of-favor growth stocks (fallen angels). For this strategy Fremont Investment Advisors (FIA) employs Relative Value Discipline, which is composed of two valuation disciplines: Relative Dividend Yield (RDY) and Relative Price-to-Sales Ratio (RPSR). Past performance does not guarantee future results.

All included accounts have substantially the same investment objectives and policies and are managed in a substantially similar manner. Some of the accounts are not subject to certain investment limitations, diversification requirements, and other restrictions imposed by federal securities and tax laws that, if applied, may have affected performance results.

Time-weighted total returns reflect both realized and unrealized capital gains and losses, income (including accrued

Performance as of September 30, 2002

	YTD	1-Year	3-Year	Annualized Since Inception**	1998**	Annual Returns 1999	2000	2001
*New Era Strategy Composite**	−36.4%	−29.1%	−14.2%	−3.8%	18.1%	40.6%	−1.2%	−18.4%
S&P 500 Index	−28.2%	−20.5%	−12.9%	−6.1%	10.4%	21.0%	−9.1%	−11.9%
Dow Jones Industrial Average Index	−23.1%	−12.5%	−8.2%	−2.0%	4.2%	27.2%	−4.7%	−5.4%
NASDAQ Index	−39.7%	−21.5%	−24.5%	−10.4%	17.1%	85.6%	−39.3%	−21.1%

*Composite Returns are gross of fees and expenses.

**Inception Date is 7/31/98.

Source: Data from Fremont Investment Advisors

dividends), and reinvestment of dividends. Returns include all accounts managed by FIA in the New Era Value style. Account returns are dollar-weighted based on the beginning-of-the-period market values. Results are on a monthly basis. Returns are geometrically linked to determine the annual return. Investment return and principal value will vary so that a gain or loss may occur upon the sale of shares. Investment performance shown herein does not include the deduction of advisory fees, or other expenses that a client would have paid or actually paid.

Advisory fees are described in Part II of the Form ADV for FIA, which may be obtained upon request.

Performance returns are compared to those of an unmanaged market index, which is considered to be a relevant comparison to the portfolio. The Dow Jones Industrial Average, the S&P 500 Index, and the NASDAQ are unmanaged indexes which are considered representative of the stock market in general. It is not possible to invest directly in an index. The inclusion of out-of-favor growth stocks, including technology, may create greater volatility of returns than a portfolio solely comprised of traditional value securities. The investment return and principal value of an investment will fluctuate so that an investor's shares, when redeemed, may be worth more or less than their original cost.

APPENDIX B:
ESTEE LAUDER—TWELVE FUNDAMENTAL FACTORS
Estee Lauder Companies, Inc. Valuation Factors

Qualitative (2 of 3)	Y	N	Quantitative (5 of 9)	Y	N
Buggy Whip	X		Sales/Revenue Growth		X
Franchise or Niche Value	X		Operating Margins	X	
Top Management and Board of Directors	X		Relative P/E	X	
			Positive Free Cash Flow	X	
			Dividend Coverage and Growth	NA	NA
			Asset Turnover		X
			Investment in Business/ROIC	X	
			Equity Leverage	X	
			Financial Risk	X	
Overall Assessment: PASS					

QUALITATIVE APPRAISAL

1. **The Buggy Whip Factor—Pass**   In light of the secular growth trend in personal care products, the risk that skin care, makeup, fragrance, or hair care products will become obsolete any time soon seems pretty remote. Indeed, social pressure to improve one's appearance has existed for centuries. Expeditions for the fountain of youth have been launched by both adventurers and lab scientists. Recognizing and capitalizing on humanity's quest to appear more attractive, beauty and cosmetics companies have been able to turn their products into near-necessities in the minds of consumers all around the globe.

   Looking forward, the aging of the baby boom generation will continue to create a rising tide of demand for products that help maintain one's beauty and youthful appearance. As a leading player in cosmetics, skin care, fragrance, and hair care, we believe that Estee Lauder Companies ("Estee") is in the sweet spot and will benefit greatly from these trends.

   With that said, there is one "buggy whip factor" that needs to be considered when dealing with the skin care and makeup business. Newer technologies and continual product improvements can make older vintage products a lot less appealing and, in the extreme case, even make them obsolete. Here again, however, we believe that Estee's fifty-year track record of creating technologically advanced and superior-quality products ensures that it will stay on the cutting edge of cosmetic technology.

2. **Franchise or Niche Value—Pass**   Estee is a clear leader in the industry. The company was founded in 1946 and has since become a global leader, operating in over 120 countries and territories around the world. Its products are classified into the four basic categories of

skin care, makeup, fragrance, and hair care. Its stable of brands has grown from five to sixteen over the past twelve years and includes established household names like Clinique, Aramis, and Donna Karan, as well as younger upstarts such as M.A.C., Stila, and Origins. With unmatched diversity in terms of brand names, geography, and product categories, we believe that Estee's brand equity is among the strongest of any consumer company. While it is not easy to quantify, brand equity has created strong consumer loyalty and has allowed Estee to charge premium prices for its products.

In terms of market share, Estee continues to dominate the cosmetic counters in high-end department stores around the world. Specifically, Estee claims a 50 percent and growing share of the U.S. department stores in which it chooses to operate, a similarly strong 30 percent share in Japan, and a steady 24 percent share of the European beauty market. As one of the larger and more important vendors to department stores (cosmetics are very attractive products that keep customers coming back into the stores regularly), Estee is able to leverage its dominance into favorable terms (i.e., sacrifice less and still get the premium real estate/counter space).

3. **Top Management and Board of Directors—Pass**
The company traces its origins back to the 1930s, when Estee Lauder first started her beauty career by selling skin care products formulated by her Hungarian uncle. In 1944, with the help of her husband, she set up her first office in Queens, New York, and by the 1950s she was selling her line of products in high-profile department stores like Neiman Marcus, I. Magnin, and Saks. The initial public offering occurred in November 1995.

Estee's management team is highly regarded within the industry. They have depth of experience, a global perspective, and are known for their ability to build and manage brands. In terms of depth, more than one-third of the company's fourteen officers have at least twenty-five years of experience in the business. The remainder has an average of thirteen years of experience. With regard to brand building, Estee has been highly successful in identifying current lifestyles/trends and establishing brands that speak to those qualities (e.g., holistic, therapeutic, mainstream, or hip). Perhaps even more important, Estee supports the trend or theme with the delivery of high-quality products that build loyal customers. As the CEO put it at a recent presentation, "While advertising starts the conversation with consumers, the challenge lies in keeping the dialogue going."

Leonard A. Lauder has been with the company since 1958. He is currently Chairman of the Company, having served as the CEO from 1995 to 2000. Since 1958, Mr. Lauder has held a variety of positions, including thirteen years as President. Before joining the company, Mr. Lauder served as an officer in the United States Navy. He is credited as being the driving force behind the company's international expansion and growing portfolio of brands.

Fred Langhammer became CEO in January 2000 after serving as President from 1995 to 2000. Before that, he was the Chief Operating Officer. Mr. Langhammer brings significant international experience, having previously served as President of Japanese operations and Managing Director of German operations.

Ronald S. Lauder is Chairman of Clinique Laboratories and Estee Lauder International. Mr. Lauder has been serving in various capacities since 1964, but he did leave the company for a short time in the mid-1980s to serve as Deputy Assistant Secretary of Defense for European and NATO affairs and as U.S. Ambassador to Austria.

While acknowledging that the Lauder family has a significant amount of management and voting control over the company, management's commitment to creating shareholder value is demonstrated by their track record. The company ensures that management's interests stay aligned with those of the shareholders through the use of performance-based compensation. From a review of last year's proxy statement, key executive employment agreements include common stock option grants carrying an exercise price of $40.50 (a rough 20 percent premium to the current price). Including restricted stock and cash bonuses, variable compensation amounts to more than 50 percent of total compensation.

QUANTITATIVE APPRAISAL

4. **Sales/Revenue Growth—Fail**   Estee fails on this factor because slower sales growth has been the primary driver behind the recent decline in the stock (and the reason it is buyable under our discipline). While acknowledging that recent trends have been less than stellar, these trends are more reflective of the macroeconomic environment than any degradation in the company's competitive position or industry fundamentals. Based on a review of competitors' sales trends, the decline at Estee was pretty much in-line with the average. Looking forward, we believe that a re-acceleration of sales into the mid-to-high single digits is very achievable.

Prior to the September 11, 2001, terrorist attacks, the U.S. economy was already in a tailspin. Sales for Estee and the rest of the retail industry reflected that fact. After September 11, a painful economic situation turned into an excruciating one. In the ensuing six months, Estee's sales growth slowed further as U.S. retailers and department stores became highly focused on managing their limited cash in the face of an uncertain outlook for consumer spending. Furthermore, because Estee used duty-free stores to distribute the majority of its fragrance products, it also felt the pinch of international travel coming to a halt. To put some numbers to it, Estee's annual sales growth had averaged 8 percent during its first six years as a public company. Its sales growth had already slowed to 5.5 percent in the fiscal year ending in June 2001. Following September 11, sales were expected grow a meager 1 to 2 percent.

The outlook, however, is much brighter. In fiscal 2003, sales could re-accelerate to 5 to 6 percent with a slight improvement in the economic picture. U.S. macroeconomic data has been consistently above expectations since early February. With the passage of six months since September 11, mall traffic seems to be on the mend and consumer confidence is skyrocketing on the back of an improving employment outlook. Finally, while we don't anticipate a strong rebound in international travel activity, at the margin, it should become less of a drag as time reduces travel anxieties related to September 11.

Looking longer term, we believe that Estee can get back to 7 to 9 percent sales growth by (1) continuing its record of innovation, (2) leveraging its marketing and brand savvy (e.g., aggressive in-store promotions and additional direct-operated stores), and (3) using Estee's proven blueprint of buying promising brands and leveraging them across its global platform.

5. **Operating Margins—Pass** Most recently, Estee's pre-tax operating margin has been trending down, as the company was unable, and in certain cases unwilling, to cut expenses in the face of slowing sales. Moving forward, we believe that re-accelerating sales and an increased focus on costs will reverse the trend. In fiscal 2001, Estee's pre-tax operating margin slipped to a low 10.5 percent from more than 11 percent during the previous two years. This slippage reflected (1) the

continued build-out of the company's direct-operated stores and (2) management's commitment to keeping its brand cachet strong despite a weaker sales environment (i.e., high advertising and promotion expense as a percent of sales).

With respect to industry comparisons, Estee's pre-tax margin still remains above average when compared to other makeup and skin care companies (Revlon, Elizabeth Arden, and Avon). In fact, within that group, only Avon, with its lower-cost direct sales model, shows a higher pre-tax margin at 14 percent (versus Estee's 10.5 percent).

While we are not expecting a significant improvement on the expense front in the current fiscal year (which ends in June 2002), we do believe that Estee has several initiatives in place that should allow more of its 79 percent gross margin to flow to the bottom line in fiscal 2003. The current areas of focus are (1) reducing the number of SKUs (i.e., the bar codes used to track inventories and reorders), (2) taking a more unified and cost-effective approach to brand management, and (3) improving supply chain management systems. These efforts, along with right-sizing other expenses to a slower projected sales environment in fiscal 2003, make us confident in the company's ability and desire to improve its operating margins over time. Meanwhile, for the reasons already discussed in section four, ramping sales could also provide a boost to margins.

6. **Relative P/E—Pass**   Estee's forward P/E ratio is well below historic peak levels on both an absolute and relative basis. At $34, Estee's shares trade at 28.2 times calendar 2002 earnings estimates and 24.7 times calendar 2003 earnings. This translates into a 22 percent and 19 percent premium to the market multiple for each of those years, respectively. This level is well below the

Estee Lauder P/E Relative to S&P

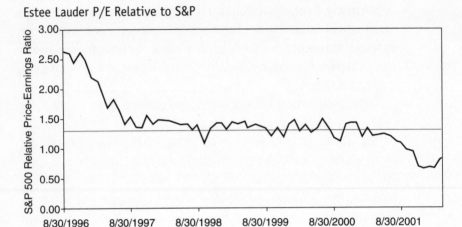

Source: Data from FactSet.

average 50 percent premium awarded to Estee's shares since 1996. On trailing earnings, Estee looks even cheaper with a current relative multiple of 84 percent and an average of 130 percent. Finally, comparing Estee to a customized set of peer companies, the stock also looks cheap, trading at a slight 13 percent premium to the group versus an historical average of closer to 35 percent.

7. **Positive Free Cash Flow—Pass** Estee has generated positive net operating cash flows in each year since coming public. In fact, net operating cash flows have grown at an impressive 15 percent compound annual growth rate since 1996. In recent years, much of the free cash flow has been spent on building up Estee's base of direct-operated stores, which is reflected in the 25 percent compound annual growth in capital expenditures.

Looking at the recent past, Estee's cash flow growth has typically outpaced earnings growth. In fiscal 2001, however, slowing economic conditions (and retail sales) caused inventories to build up, which in turn caused net operating cash flows to shrink by 31 percent. In the first half of fiscal 2002, with retailers destocking their inventories, working capital levels have begun to fall. With cash flows improving again, Estee has managed to bring its assets/equity ratio to under 2.0 times for the first time in the company's history.

8. **Dividend Coverage and Growth—NA**   With historically strong earnings growth and a low 0.6 percent dividend yield, Estee is viewed more as a reasonably valued, recovering growth story than a traditional high-dividend-yielding value stock. Therefore, the current dividend is not a meaningful part of the total return analysis. All that said, we believe the current dividend is secure given the company's strong positive operating cash flow.

9. **Asset Turnover—Fail**   While in line with its competitors, Estee's asset turns have been slowing. During the past five fiscal years, Estee's asset turnover has averaged 1.59 times; however, that figure masks the underlying deterioration which occurred over the period. When viewed by fiscal year, the ratio has actually fallen from a peak of 1.83 times in fiscal 1997 to a current low of 1.47 times as the company experienced a significant growth in the number of brands it manages. Also impacting asset turns and inventory levels was the company's international growth. The number of SKUs ballooned to 14,000 as packaging requirements differed by brand, not to mention locale. Given this explanation, we believe that asset turns have stabilized and do not expect material deterioration from these levels.

10. **Investment in Business/ROIC—Pass**   While Estee's return on invested capital (or ROIC) has declined from 21 percent in 2001 to a projected 18 percent in fiscal 2002, it is still comfortably above its estimated weighted average cost of capital (roughly 8 percent). In our view, the

downtrend is reflective of both temporary and longer-term structural issues at Estee. The temporary issue would be the slowdown in sales and resultant temporary working capital inefficiencies, while the longer-term structural shift is due to the company's migration toward a more capital-intense direct-operated store model.

Estee has a strong track record of investment in R&D and advertising to support its brands. Specifically, research and development has grown from 1.0 percent of sales in 1996 to 1.3 percent of sales in fiscal 2001. While not broken out separately, we believe the company's commitment to building and managing its brands is unquestionable. This "managing for the long haul" mentality contributed to a relatively high level of advertising and promotion expense given the current softer sales environment.

11. **Equity Leverage—Pass**   We believe that the company has built an unparalleled amount of brand equity and has also been successful in creating value through acquisitions. The company's blueprint has been, and continues to be, buying promising young brands and leveraging them across its global platform—a formula that works. To name a few, the company acquired M.A.C. in 1994, La Mer and Bobbi Brown in 1995, and Jane and Aveda in 1997. Probably the most telling statistic with regard to creating value through acquisitions is the fact that as Estee transitions to FASB 142 "Accounting for Goodwill," it will be taking a paltry $20 million (3 percent) impairment charge on the more than $700 million in Goodwill it has on its balance sheet.

12. **Financial Risk—Pass**   While Estee has a long track record of uninterrupted growth, the company has been careful to maintain a fortress-like balance sheet. In

recent years, free cash flow has been used (among other things) to reduce debt, as evidenced by the decline in the company's assets-to-equity ratio from 2.4 times at the end of fiscal 1998 to a low 1.9 times at the end of fiscal 2001. Measured another way, the debt-to-equity market value has declined from about 65 percent to 40 percent over the same period despite recent declines in Estee's market capitalization. Bottom line, financial leverage is not considered a significant issue at Estee.

Joseph Cuenco, CFA
April 12, 2002

APPENDIX C:
EMC—TWELVE FUNDAMENTAL FACTORS

EMC Valuation Factors

Qualitative (2 of 3)	Y	N	Quantitative (5 of 9)	Y	N
Buggy Whip	X		Sales/Revenue Growth		X
Franchise or Niche Value	X		Operating Margins		X
Top Management and Board of Directors	X		Relative P/E	X	
			Positive Free Cash Flow	X	
			Dividend Coverage and Growth	NA	NA
			Asset Turnover	X	
			Investment in Business/ROIC	X	
			Equity Leverage	X	
			Financial Risk	X	
Overall Assessment: PASS					

QUALITATIVE APPRAISAL

1. **The Buggy Whip Factor—Pass** The need for storage and, more importantly, storage management can be summed up best by the now-famous University of California at Berkeley study which estimated that it has taken the entire history of humanity through 2000 to accumulate 15 exabytes (1 exabyte $= 10^{18}$ bytes[1]) of information. By the middle of 2003, the second 15 exabytes will have been created. This level of exponential growth will drive storage spending growth, excluding software, to outpace server spending growth by a factor of three to one. Dataquest projects storage spending, excluding software, will approach $60.4 billion by 2004, a CAGR[2] of 18.4 percent. In contrast, server spending is projected to approach, $87.8 billion, or grow at an annualized rate of 6.6 percent. Spending on storage, as a percentage of total dollars spent on computing systems according to a recent Merrill Lynch study, will move from 25 percent storage and 75 percent servers to eventually 75 percent storage and 25 percent servers.

   So what are the fundamental drivers behind the growth in data and the need for storage? Recent studies point to several areas behind the growth in storage.

   ▌ E-mail is generally thought to be the first "killer" application for the Internet. A recent study by Midrange Performance Group indicates the average size of any e-mail message, including attachments, now exceeds 50 kilobytes and is rising. As voice mail and video mail merge with e-mail, the requirements of e-mail storage will be pushed well beyond current levels. IDC estimates there were over 10 billion e-mail messages sent worldwide on an average day. This is expected to grow to 35 billion by 2005, a 29 percent CAGR.

I Recent studies indicate 85 to 90 percent of all health care information is stored on paper or film. An X-ray generally consumes 12 megabytes of storage. According to research, if a hospital performs 200 X-rays per bed per year, a 500-bed hospital will generate 100,000 X-rays per year, resulting in 1.2 terabytes of storage. Backing up and archiving this data triples this storage requirement.

I Mission critical applications such as ERP,[3] CRM,[4] and SCM[5] continue to be broadly deployed. In addition, data warehousing, which combines different databases into one, enhances the power of enterprise applications and further drives the demand for storage. The applications and warehousing markets are projected to grow 13 percent and 26 percent, respectively.

I "Killer applications" include digital photography, video streaming, set-top boxes and personal TVs, video conferencing, and MP3s. UC Berkeley estimates that 2,700 photographs are taken every second around the world, annually generating the digital equivalent of 800,000 terabytes. As photos and videos move to a digital format, households will have to learn to manage terabytes of data. Video streaming is also becoming more pervasive in the corporate landscape as executives utilize it for everything from employee education and sales training to marketing.

However, the solution to more data is simply not more storage. Storage requirements are many and complex. Customers want easy and fast access to large volumes of primary data relating to customers, employees, financial performance, and so on. Backup and replication of data is essential, with no tolerance for loss of data. Redundant copies of databases must be at different locations to avoid loss of data during a power outage or a more severe catastrophe, such as the tragedy of September 11, 2001.

Storage capacity must be easy and timely to scale in a cost-effective manner. Lastly, ease of use is essential, as is fast, user-friendly, enterprise-wide access to multiple copies of critical data. What this illustrates is that storage is more than just hardware. It is now estimated that hardware comprises less than 20 percent of the total cost of ownership (TCO) of information storage compared to 75 percent just a few years back. The 80 percent non-hardware TCO breakdown is based on systems integration, storage software, storage networking, utilization, support and training, and other costs of management. As an example, assuming data growth doubles every year, a company that currently has 1.5 terabytes of data will have 192 terabytes in seven years. According to IDC, managing this information in three years will require thirty-six people at an average cost of $100,000 per person, or a total cost of $3.6 million. If the company deploys networked information storage and software, IDC projects headcount and personnel costs will remain relatively flat, even as storage capacity scales. Therefore, instead of needing thirty-six people to manage 192 terabytes, the company will need only four people for a total cost of $400,000. This not only equates to $3.2 million in cost savings but, in addition, the IT employee can be redeployed to revenue-generating activities which would have been an opportunity cost without the savings outlined.

Storage is becoming more complex and has moved beyond the simple, direct, attached model to the more complex, networked model that has applications layered on top to increase utilization and efficiency. EMC is the market leader in networked storage and is leading the evolution in this branch of technology.

2. **Franchise or Niche Value—Pass** EMC is *the* market leader in storage—hardware and software. Though competing against the likes of IBM, Hitachi, Hewlett-

Packard, Network Appliance, and Sun Microsystems (companies with greater resources and larger market capitalizations), EMC has remained the leader in storage for one simple reason: EMC understands storage. EMC's pure play status in storage has facilitated its lead in marketing the latest product innovations, developing a large installed base of enterprise accounts, and building a sales force and support infrastructure that is considered the best in the industry.

One of the primary concerns in the marketplace today is competition from the likes of IBM, Hitachi, Hewlett-Packard, and Sun Microsystems. The fear is that aggressive pricing will erode EMC's market share and margins as these large, well-capitalized companies emphasize storage as a greater percentage of their business mix. However, as previously discussed, storage is becoming more complex. The majority of the cost of storage lies in the implementation, integration, software, support, and services functions rather than hardware. Quoting a leading industry analyst from the Enterprise Storage Group, "EMC understands it's not about the box." Hewlett-Packard and Sun Microsystems are sourcing their storage "box" needs from Hitachi. Hitachi's distribution model is questionable given they are or will be competing against their own customers, Sun and Hewlett, and these companies are in the process of developing their own software platforms. In addition, IBM and Hitachi recently announced an ambiguous collaboration to develop a common approach to virtualization.[6] This introduces another level of complexity into the Hitachi model of sourcing to other OEMs and calls into question IBM's software proposition, StorageTank, which is expected to compete with EMC's Auto IS initiative. It is not clear how this collaboration will provide momentum behind the Common Information Model (CIM) standard. CIM effectively seeks to standardize how management information is collected, transcribed, and presented. This in turn should enable the sharing and management of data among heterogeneous systems and devices. EMC's WideSky middleware seeks to address this problem. We are not in any way seeking to minimize the ability of IBM and Hitachi to compete effectively in the storage space. The point is that EMC, as a pure play in storage, has taken advantage of its market leadership and expertise to stay one step ahead of the competition. One of the common arguments for not choosing the EMC platform, and one highly promoted by IBM and Sun Microsystems, is that storage is not a separate purchase decision. Rather, it can be bundled with servers and mainframes. On the contrary, as Joe Tucci of EMC adroitly points out, if the trend is away from server-attached storage to network-attached storage, then storage is a separate purchase decision, particularly as the complexity rises exponentially at the network level. It is also not certain if large enterprises would want one vendor serving their computing/mission critical needs.

EMC has also taken steps to enrich its business model by re-examining its distribution strategy, addressing new markets, and emphasizing software. Late last year, EMC announced a partnership with Dell to co-brand and sell EMC's mid-range CLARiiON product. The deal gives EMC a potent distribution channel, particularly in the government, health care, and education markets. It also provides access to Dell's manufacturing know-how and working capital management, plus the opportunity to further increase its hardware-installed base. The increased hardware base should theoretically increase EMC's potential software market. To further improve sales productivity, management recently hired the consulting firm McKinsey & Co. to undertake a broad review of EMC's sales strategy and develop a lower-cost sales structure. Sharpening its focus on large enterprises and shifting other accounts to business partners such as Dell should help right-size the firm's business model, which has often been criticized as too leveraged, particularly in light of the current pricing environment. However, we would caution, one of the attributes that made EMC such a huge success was its sales force and support staff, which have been characterized by many in the industry as second to none. *We would become cautious on the stock if it became evident there was confusion at the sales level in light of a major restructuring or sales force reorganization.*

EMC's new product offering, Centera, should open an incremental market opportunity by broadening the scope of potential storage applications. The product seeks to address the storage of fixed content, content that is not typically updated, or content that is accessed sporadically and needs to be stored for an extended period of time. This category of electronic information is effectively non-mission critical data. Medical imaging files, spreadsheets, and video files are a few examples. Industry analysts estimate 50 percent of online data will be fixed content by 2005. Markets for Centera will require integration and development, with near-term contributions to the bottom line expected to be only 3 percent to the bottom line. However, the product demonstrates the ability of the company to think "outside the box."

Software will also be a major emphasis for EMC. Storage is presently 20 percent of revenues. Management has stated that storage would comprise 30 percent of revenues by 2005, with some industry experts estimating the contribution to be well above 30 percent. Software carries gross margins of 85 percent to 90 percent and EMC is the leader in the two spaces that are expected to grow the fastest: replication and storage resource management. The growth of applications under EMC's Auto

IS[7] initiative, which proactively manages storage, and the success of partnerships such as the aforementioned Dell agreement will be key to measuring EMC's success in software. *EMC is already a trusted source for software as EMC's equipment sits in the heart of some of the biggest data centers on the planet.*

EMC is in a position to lose only if the damage is self-inflicted. The company is adapting to current market conditions and its focus allows it to stay one step ahead of the competition.

3. **Top Management and Board of Directors—Pass**
   Management is facing two major hurdles in the interim which it must address in a prompt, direct, and thoughtful fashion: competition and the company's business model. The company as stated is reviewing its distribution model and has hired McKinsey to review its sales and pricing strategy. The manner in which management guides the organization through this transition will determine the company's long-term competitive position. Though change often causes disruption, the fact that management is addressing the issues should be construed as a positive. Joe Tucci is the current CEO of EMC, having joined the firm in 2000 as COO. Though lacking a technology background, his managerial skills are well-regarded and should come in handy through the current transitional period. The one major positive Mr. Tucci brings to the table is that he is an outsider with a fresh perspective. To that end, he has made some changes at the management level, most notably the recent hire of Chris Gaghan, a highly regarded storage executive who will oversee the development of EMC's storage infrastructure software, a critical component of EMC's open storage software development efforts and part of the EMC Auto IS strategy.

   EMC's Board, however, has been the subject of much criticism. As of the 2001 proxy, the Board was primarily made up of inside directors (five out of the eight were current or former employees) and two others who had close business relationships with EMC. Generally the Board must be a thoughtful, independent voice. That said, shareholders recently approved a resolution to make the majority of the firm's directors independent. This action will also result in the Audit, Compensation, and Nominating Committees being composed entirely of independent directors. Two Board seats expire in 2003 and two more in 2004. One of the changes we would like to see is an increase in the level of inside stock ownership, which currently stands at 0.32 percent of all outstanding shares. Hopefully this issue will be addressed when the committee changes occur.

Overall, a strong Board would be comforting from an investor point of view as the company transitions through some changes. However, the proactive nature of management thus far at the very least demonstrates the acknowledgment and the willingness to change even though the company is still the leader in its space.

QUANTITATIVE APPRAISAL

4. **Sales/Revenue Growth—Fail** While adjusting for the Data General acquisition in August 1999, revenues had grown at an annualized rate of 42 percent over the past five years through 2000. This was a function of a strong economy, the Internet, increased storage spending in preparation for Y2K, and EMC's market share gains. However, since peaking in 2000, revenues have fallen off sharply, declining 32 percent. Pricing, competition from Hitachi and IBM, and the weak economy have had the biggest impact on the top line.

The big question at the moment is: Has the price war between EMC, IBM, and Hitachi subsided? EMC has been aggressive in defending its market share; however, the company appears to have eased on its rhetoric of defending market share at all costs. Hitachi and IBM have eliminated the technology gap in hardware that EMC enjoyed for some time which contributed to EMC's top line and margins—EMC effectively was the only game in town. Interestingly enough, though, EMC has been investing in software, and many industry analysts believe it will be software and not hardware that will differentiate the company's products in the storage space. The price per megabyte has declined 50 percent in the last two years with EMC's hardware gross margins falling from 57 percent at their peak in the fourth quarter of 2000 to 7 percent at their trough in the third quarter of 2001. In the just-reported first quarter of 2002, hardware gross margins have rebounded to 16 percent. Overall corporate gross margins in the first quarter were 36 percent. However, investors do not believe, as some are contesting, that storage hardware is a commodity business similar to the PC business, where gross margins have been reduced to the high teens. Given the software and services component to hardware (bundling so to speak) in storage—which is in sharp contrast to the PC, where the box is effectively separate from the operating system and software—we believe margins in hardware will rebound to the mid-20 percent range once the economy recovers. In addition, as discussed, EMC's new initiatives in distribution, software, and products like Centera should at the very minimum produce a top-line growth rate that is in line with the industry.

Software will be the primary top-line driver for EMC moving forward. The secular growth rate for storage in revenues going forward, excluding software, as projected by Dataquest is estimated to be 18 percent annualized through 2005. Software is expected to grow at an annualized rate of 20 to 25 percent through 2005. Industry service revenues are projected to grow conservatively at 5 percent annualized through 2005. As of the latest reported results for EMC in the first quarter of 2002, the revenue breakdown was as follows: 57 percent storage systems or hardware, 22 percent software, and 18 percent storage services. The company is shifting its focus, targeting software to comprise 30 percent of total revenues by 2004. Software for the company has gone from 12 percent of revenues in 1999 to the latest 22 percent previously stated. Growth in software will principally be driven by the success of EMC's Auto IS initiative. The market that Auto IS seeks to address has very conservatively been estimated to grow at 25 percent annualized through 2005. The company's current software mix of SRM (storage resource management) and replication, approximately 96 percent of EMC software revenues, is projected to grow +20 percent conservatively. This is one-half the EMC story—growth in software. The other half is margins, discussed later. Some industry observers, however, believe EMC is being very conservative in its estimates for software's contribution to overall revenues. The optimists believe it will represent close to 40 to 50 percent by 2005. However, we are conservatively modeling 30 percent contribution by 2004.

EMC is initiating changes to its business model as the storage market evolves. Given the depth of the current downturn and a level of risk inherent with any sort of business mix shift, EMC is failing on this measure. However, we believe EMC is poised for growth once the economy and capital spending recover. The only question mark is, will it be at the industry growth rate of 18 percent to 20 percent or faster? Given the initiatives taken by the company thus far, we believe it will be faster.

5. **Operating Margins—Fail** Operating margins peaked in 2000 at 25.4 percent and have declined since. The company lost money in the first quarter of 2002 with margins at −11.2 percent. However, the company is trying to right-size its business model, having taken enough

expenses out of its cost structure to reduce its revenue breakeven run-rate to $1.55 billion per quarter or $6.2 billion per annum; the company's peak sales were $8.9 billion in 2000, 44 percent greater than the current run-rate. For the quarter just ended, the first quarter of 2002, the revenue run-rate was $1.3 billion. The company's margins at their peak were substantially greater than Hewlett-Packard, IBM, Sun Microsystems, and Network Appliance, a small, fast-growing company in the network storage space. However, in the current downturn, the margins are well below the companies previously mentioned. This is causing many to wonder if the company's cost structure is too high, particularly if one reviews the sales/employee metric that has been declining since peaking in 1996. However, the company as stated has undertaken a broad review of its cost structure, particularly in light of the Dell partnership and its focus on software. Assuming the top line grows at a normalized industry rate of 18 percent, operating margins should settle in the 17 percent range by 2005, with earnings per share in the $0.55 to $0.60 range. The 17 percent margin is well off the peak margins previously noted of 25 percent. Note, however, that this 17 percent normal operating margin is well above Sun Microsystem's and IBM's *peak* 2000 operating margins of 15.3 percent and 13.2 percent, respectively. However, given *current* margin levels, the company fails on this measure.

6. **Relative P/E—Pass** The company's average relative P/E over the past ten-year and five-year periods has been 1.6 times and 1.8 times the S&P 500, respectively. The lowest the company traded on a trailing twelve-month basis was in 2001 when the stock traded at 0.54 times the market. In 1995, EMC traded as low as 0.56 times the market. However, noting that we are near the bottom in terms of sales, margins, and earnings, the

relative multiple should improve with the company's profit outlook.

Earnings in a normalized environment would equate to $0.55 to $0.60 per share, assuming mid- to high-teens operating margins. The company is currently trading at 14 times "normalized earnings." However, if one backs out cash and long-term investments from the current market capitalization, the company is trading at 10 times "normalized" earnings or 0.5 times the market's 2002 earnings multiple. As the company's model evolves and margins improve, the company's earnings valuation should also improve.

7. **Positive Free Cash Flow—Pass** The company managed to earn $1.44 billion in operating cash flow, adjusted for investment income, in 2001, even though it recorded a loss in net income of $508 million. A net improvement in working capital contributed to over one-half the increase in operating cash flow. Operating cash flow per share relative to earnings per share has been steady to improving the past few years.

Working capital turnover at the company, however, has been lax. Days of sales outstanding[8] (DSOs) in early 1998 were as low as forty days; however, they have since peaked in 2001 at close to 120 days. In the most recent quarter just announced, DSOs fell to eighty-five days, well above the company target of seventy days and industry peers such as Sun Microsystems. The eighty-five days, however, is an improvement from the 120-day peak and the most recent 90-day average for the twelve months ending in March. Inventory turnover has not fared better. Though it is showing signs of improvement at sixty-three days, it is still well above Sun's twenty-eight-day average. The significant uptick in the cash conversion cycle in 2001 was probably due to the company extending generous payment terms to customers in 2001 to try and facilitate overly exuberant sales objectives.

Though reality has set in, we would still like the company to take an aggressive stance on improving its working capital turns.

8. **Dividend Coverage and Growth—NA** As EMC is an RPSR stock, it is not rated on this factor.

9. **Asset Turnover—Pass** Asset turns have been coming down over the years, dropping precipitously in the last year to 0.6, below the five-year average of 1. Several factors account for this; first, the company's cash and long-term investments have been increasing over time and presently account for over 55 percent of assets; second, the company's Data General acquisition in 1999 increased the asset base by over 20 percent; third, sales have declined by over 40 percent since peaking in 2000 when asset turns were 1; and lastly, working capital turns at the company have been below par as discussed. The greatest impact on the decline in turnover has come from the increase in the company's cash and investments balance and the decline in sales. Assuming sales growth of 15 to 20 percent for EMC and asset turns in the 0.9 to 1.0 range, the company can generate earnings in the $0.55 range.

While generally cash on hand is a good thing, too much can also depress returns. EMC's ROE, in conjunction with its ROA, has been declining over the years as investment in capacity and the rising cash balance have produced declining returns. However, with the shift in focus emphasizing software, an increased level of investment or an acquisition in this space, provided the returns were adequate, would be viewed positively. The company, it should be pointed out, has been investing in start-ups that concentrate on storage.

10. **Investment in Business/ROIC—Pass** The company's return on invested capital has been declining since 1995

as after-tax EBIT growth has been declining relative to net assets employed. Again, however, this is a function of cash and long-term investments constituting a sizable portion of assets employed. Regardless, the company's investments in R&D, in particular software, private equity investments, and acquisitions such as Data General, have generated returns in the form of the Auto IS initiative and the CLARiiON product line. That said, given the level of well-capitalized competition, EMC should not deter from its R&D focus. On an absolute dollar basis, EMC in 2001 invested $929 million in R&D, compared to Veritas' $241 million. However, both of these numbers are inconsequential when compared to IBM's $5.3 billion and Sun Microsystems' $2 billion R&D budgets. As a percentage of sales, EMC's R&D budget has averaged 9 percent, Veritas has averaged 15 percent, Sun Microsystems 11 percent, and IBM 6 percent. EMC's clear advantage is its focus on storage and its ability to leverage its sales force and R&D initiatives to further penetrate its large installed customer base.

11. **Equity Leverage—Pass** The equity leverage ratio has been declining the past few years. However, so has asset turnover, which has led to a declining ROE, with the exception of 2000 when margins rose 400 basis points to offset the declining asset turnover. That said, if the company's software initiatives are successful, the ROE should improve and the company will have the opportunity to reinvest through higher R&D and/or acquisitions/private investments.

12. **Financial Risk—Pass** The company's balance sheet is clean with no long-term debt. In fact, the company has $2.36 per share or $5.2 billion of cash and investments on the balance sheet. In terms of off-balance sheet items, the company has operating leases totaling $795 million and purchase obligations for 2002 of $847 million related

to manufacturing and non-manufacturing-related goods. Purchase orders generally are cancelable without penalty; however, certain vendor agreements do provide for percentage-based cancellation fees. In terms of operating leases, the payments are well staggered with $216 million due this year, $282 million over the next one- to three-year periods, $124 million over periods four to five, and $113 million after five years. The company generates adequate cash flow from operations and has enough cash on hand to meet these needs.

Harshal Shah, CFA
June 30, 2002

NOTES

1. Byte is the equivalent of a single character.
2. Compound annual growth rate.
3. Enterprise resource planning.
4. Client relationship management.
5. Sales contact management.
6. Virtualization allows for the creation of a single pool of "virtual" storage that communicates logically with different operating systems, applications, and storage devices.
7. Auto IS: Automated information storage.
8. Days of sales outstanding refers to how long (measured in number of days) it takes for a company to collect its receivables. DSO = $365/((Sales * 4)/$ Average Accounts Receivable for the last two quarters).

APPENDIX D:
WALT DISNEY—TWELVE
FUNDAMENTAL FACTORS
The Walt Disney Company (DIS) Valuation Factors

Qualitative (2 of 3)	Y	N	Quantitative (5 of 9)	Y	N
Buggy Whip	X		Sales/Revenue Growth	X	
Franchise or Niche Value	X		Operating Margins	X	
Top Management and Board of Directors	X		Relative P/E	X	
			Positive Free Cash Flow	X	
			Dividend Coverage and Growth	X	
			Asset Turnover		X
			Investment in Business/ROIC		X
			Equity Leverage		X
			Financial Risk	X	
Overall Assessment: PASS					

QUALITATIVE APPRAISAL

1. **Buggy Whip—Pass** Disneyland—"The Happiest Place on Earth."

   "The Happiest Place on Earth," as all of the Disney Parks have come to be known, attracts parents and grandparents alike, who share their Disney childhood experiences with their children and grandchildren. From the cradle to the grave, Disney literally continues to capture the "mind share" of at least three family generations: children, parents, and grandparents. This is evidenced by the growth of theme park attendance at Walt Disney World and Disneyland combined, which has grown at an annual rate of 3.6 percent since 1972.

   The growth in theme park attendance is not a localized phenomenon—50 percent of the visitors to Disney World and 25 percent of the visitors to Disneyland arrive via air travel. Of the visitors to both parks, foreign tourists comprise 30 percent of Disney World's attendance and 17 percent of Disneyland's attendance. Unlike other parks that service a specific geographic region, Disney's theme parks are a point of destination. This is quite impressive considering the cost of a four-day vacation for a family of four to Walt Disney World is estimated to average $3,000 to $4,000. In contrast, the cost of attending a regional theme park is on average $150 to $175. In 2001, Disney's five theme parks led all North American theme parks in attendance. Disney's share of attendance of the top ten domestic theme parks in 2001 was 71 percent. On a worldwide basis, Disney's share of attendance of the top twenty global theme parks was 55 percent in 2001.

   In addition to its theme parks, Disney's content, in the form of animation, has played an integral role in the expansion and development of the Disney brand. Blockbuster movie hits such as *The Lion King* have helped build brand equity as royalty streams are developed from home video sales, consumer product sales, and the sale of music CDs, video games, and theme park attractions.

Disney is one of the most recognizable consumer brands in the world. It is a concept that is difficult to replicate and one that continues to thrive. On this basis, Disney passes the Buggy Whip factor.

2. **Franchise or Niche Value—Pass** Disney's business model, structured toward leveraging the company's content assets through its own distribution channels, has translated into increased brand awareness and franchise value. The strength of the Disney franchise can best be demonstrated by a recent brand equity study which concluded that 1.2 billion consumers have used at least one Disney product over the last 12 months. This is roughly 20 percent of the world's population of 6 billion people.

Disney has four operating business segments: Theme Parks and Resorts, Media Networks, Studio Entertainment, and Consumer Products. The two divisions that embody Disney and are essential to maintaining and growing the value of the Disney brand are Studio Entertainment and Theme Parks and Resorts. Studio Entertainment produces and distributes live action films, animated films, and animated programming for television, home videos, stage plays, and musical recordings. The Theme Parks and Resorts division is comprised of Walt Disney World, Disneyland, international theme parks, and the Disney Cruise Line.

Disney's Theme Parks and Resorts division funds a large portion of the company's growth initiatives in content and distribution. The Theme Parks division contributes 26 percent of total company sales and 32 percent of operating income. Though the Theme Parks business is a fairly mature business, revenues and operating income are expected to grow 6 percent and 7 percent, respectively, as the company continues to successfully invest in new and existing parks. Evidence of Disney's success in building this franchise is the company's ability to turn the parks into destination resorts. As Disney builds hotels and other attractions around the parks, a visit to the park becomes a vacation rather than a one-day outing. Disney's resort properties account for 30 percent of Theme Parks' revenues. The value of the Theme Park franchise is further illustrated by the company's successful international expansion efforts. Due to the high fixed cost involved in building and maintaining a park or a resort, financing becomes a major issue. However, Disney's success with its theme park operations gives the company flexibility in this area. Their options include franchising or licensing parks or using external financing to fund the project. For example, at Tokyo Disneyland the company made no investment, but rather signed a management contract providing for revenue sharing as a percentage of the resort's gross revenues from admissions, hotel occupancy, food and beverage, and so on. The company, through the management contract, is not liable for any financing or marginal financial risk and has the opportunity to maintain the quality of the Disney brand and build the value of the brand as it receives exposure to another market. Hong Kong Disneyland, a $4.7 billion project to be completed by 2005, is a partnership between Disney and the Hong Kong government. Disney will receive management and licensing fees as well as a 43 percent equity stake in exchange for a $320 million investment in 2004 and use of the brand name. A 7 percent investment in Hong Kong Disneyland for a 43 percent equity stake and licensing fees illustrates the power of the Disney brand and the company's success in growing its Theme Park business.

Disney's Studio Entertainment business is the cornerstone of the Disney franchise. A large portion of the firm's brand value is derived from the division's animated film library and its ability to successfully manage and produce new animated films, animated TV programming, and, to a certain extent, live action feature films. An example of some of the animated classics in the company's vault are *Snow White & the Seven Dwarfs*, *Cinderella*, *The Jungle Book*, *The Lion King*, *Bambi*, and *101 Dalmatians*. The success of these timeless classics can be leveraged by distributing related content through the channels Disney owns. Products can be sold and licensed through the company's Consumer Products division, attractions can be developed for Disney theme parks, home videos of the movie can be released for retail sale at a later date, and a straight-to-video sequel can be marketed. The advertising costs to promote and market the film can be directed through the company's various media outlets in the company's Media Networks segment. This segment also provides additional programming opportunities for the films themselves. An example of Disney's success in animation is the 1994 release of *The Lion King*, which generated revenues from the box office alone of $772 million. *Tarzan*, released in 1999, generated a fraction of the box office revenues produced by *The Lion King;* however, through ancillary sales revenues from *Tarzan* thus far have totaled $850 million. A large portion of this success can be attributed to the home entertainment market, a significant cash cow. While a movie, either animated or live action, might be losing money after its theatrical release, it can still reach a break-even point once it is released into the home video market. The home video market generally accounts for 40 to 50 percent of a film's gross revenue and the majority of a film's profits. The addition of syndication and other ancillary revenues can substantially lift a film's profits and revenues, as evidenced by *Tarzan*.

Disney has also developed a royalty stream off its vaunted library of animated film classics. The company has segmented the film collection into two categories: Gold and Platinum. The twenty-five titles under the Gold Collection will remain in retail circulation indefinitely, while the ten Platinum Collection titles will rotate into retail circulation once every ten years. In this way, the company avoids diluting the value of the library.

The division hit a very rough patch in 2000, generating operating profits of only $80 million on segment operating margins of 1.3 percent, as film production costs went awry and home video revenues decelerated from their peak of $3.7 billion in 1997 to $2.6 billion in 2000. The performance of Disney's in-house animation films has also been below average as the company stressed quantity over quality in the late 1990s. The company's return to somewhat-respectable margins of 4.3 percent in 2001 was largely the result of cost cutting and the company's partnership with Pixar, which produced such hits as *Toy Story*, *Toy Story 2*, *A Bug's Life*, and most recently *Monsters, Inc.* This is a critical relationship and one to watch as Pixar's co-production agreement with Disney ends in 2006 after the release of three additional films. Pixar films contributed 47 percent of the segment's operating income in 2001. Disney's animation department, however, seems to be at an inflection point. In just seven weeks the animation department's latest release, *Lilo & Stitch*, has generated over $137 million in box office revenues.

The value of the Studio Entertainment division is best illustrated through the profit contribution of its two primary segments—Home Video and Syndication. These two segments alone accounted for 19 percent of the firm's operating income in 2000. The Studio Entertainment segment is on the mend as management focuses on improving returns and the quality of its animation. Investors are expected to become positive on the stock once a definitive turn at the division is evident.

Disney's Media Networks division is the largest contributor to the company in both revenues and operating income. The segment's margins are second only to Theme Parks' margins. In 2001, Media Networks accounted for 39 percent of the firm's revenues and 46 percent of its profits. The division can be thought of as the distribution arm of the company. Its primary purpose is to serve as an extension and enforcer for the Disney brand, production, distribution, and the licensing of programming.

The division is broken into two segments: Broadcasting and Cable. Under Broadcasting, the company's television operation produces programming that is distributed globally to broadcast networks, cable and satellite operators, and domestic and international syndicates under the Walt Disney Television, Buena Vista Television, Touchstone Television, and Miramax brands. The company's ABC Television Network and the company-owned television stations reach 24 percent of the U.S. television households. When its 255 affiliated stations are included, that figure reaches 99.9 percent.

Disney's primary Cable assets include the Disney Channel, ABC Family, and ESPN. Disney, however, is making further investments in cable to expand its presence, as evidenced by the Fox Family Worldwide purchase in 2001 and the introduction of two new cable channels, Toon Disney in 1998 and Soap Net in 2000. Soap Net and Toon Disney are great illustrations of a low-cost strategy to leverage existing ABC and Disney Animation programming. Riding on ESPN's success (ESPN accounts for greater than 60 percent of Cable's operating income), Disney has been able to negotiate favorable terms for its remaining cable networks during contract renewal discussions with the cable MSOs (multiple system operators). ESPN has been able to command 20 percent annual escalators, leading ESPN to the highest affiliate fee of any national cable network. While Disney should be commended for maximizing ESPN's brand value, it should be noted the cable MSOs and satellite operators are not too happy with the company's posturing at the negotiating table. In this environment it should be noted that Fox Sports secured the rights to broadcast Major League Baseball playoff games and NASCAR racing from ESPN/ABC in 2001. The relationship with the MSOs is one that bears close scrutiny, particularly in light of financing issues that might moderate the growth prospects of these entities.

Within Disney, however, the one segment that is continually scrutinized is Broadcasting, and in particular the ABC Television Network. In 2000, the ABC Network generated 15 percent of Disney's operating profits. In 2001, the contribution was down to 6 percent and, in 2002, the Network is expected to produce a loss in excess of $500 million. Advertising is the lifeblood of Broadcasting and generally accounts for 30 percent of the company's profits. Poor ratings at ABC have exacerbated an already difficult advertising climate suffering from the weak economy. A lack of investment in programming, which was unfortunately masked by the success of *Who Wants to Be a Millionaire* in 2000, has come back to haunt the network. It is estimated that 75 percent of the Broadcasting segment's operating income growth in 2000 can be directly attributed to *Millionaire*. A great majority of its profits reside in the syndication of popular broadcast network shows. Unfortunately for ABC, they have not had a major hit in syndication since *Home Improvement* in 1995. Expectations are low for ABC; however, Susan Lyne, the new head of ABC Entertainment, hopes to make an impact this fall with seven new shows for prime time, the most new shows of the four big networks. In addition, ABC signed on HBO to develop shows for the network starting in 2003. HBO is coming off a string of successes with *The Sopranos, Six*

Feet Under, and *Everybody Loves Raymond*. The economics of the business are such that one hit show can turn around the network's fortunes.

While ABC poses a near-term challenge, overall, the Media Networks division possesses strong growth assets in ESPN and the Disney Channel. The ESPN properties alone are now worth more than the $19.6 billion Disney paid for all of Capital Cities/ABC in 1996.

Disney's Consumer Products division contributes 10 percent to the company's top line and operating income. The division provides an opportunity to maximize and extend the Disney brand. Though there are 124 characters in the company's portfolio, *Winnie the Pooh* and *Mickey Mouse* account for 66 percent of all licensed merchandise revenues. Licensing, in fact, represents 75 percent of the division's operating income. At its peak, the company had 4,000 licenses. As part of the restructuring effort led by Andy Mooney, the new president of Consumer Products hired from Nike, the division is reducing the number of licenses to a maximum 2,000.

Better product quality, product sell-through, and point of sale displays will improve the profitability of the division. However, to broaden brand awareness and grow the top line, the division will have to do a much better job of leveraging Disney's successful efforts in content. Disney Interactive, which makes up 7 percent of the division's profits, develops video games and is an excellent example of Disney's product extension strategy. The success of *Who Wants to Be a Millionaire* was immediately followed by *Millionaire* video games. Consumer Products provides a means to leverage Disney's strength in delivering quality content. Though not expected to be a major growth contributor, the division can help promote the Disney brand with the right strategy. Under Andy Mooney, the division finally seems to be on the right track.

Disney is a formidable franchise. As outlined earlier, the company has shifted from a pure growth mode to a more focused, operational approach that should re-energize the franchise and increase the earnings power of the company, particularly as the economy rebounds. On this basis, we pass the company on the Niche Value factor.

3. **Top Management—Pass** From 1980 to 1990, Disney's annualized return to a shareholder lucky enough to hold the stock was 24.4 percent. This outpaced, by a healthy margin, the S&P 500's annualized return of 13.9 percent. However, from 1990 to July 2002, Disney's stock has appreciated at an annualized rate of only 7.3 percent, lagging the S&P 500's annualized return of 11.5 percent. So, the question is: Did Michael Eisner, Disney's CEO, get lucky in the mid-1980s when home videos and cable were just catching on and a strong economy was driving growth at the Theme Parks division?

There's no question that circumstances helped Disney's and Mr. Eisner's performance. However, critics should also note that Eisner maximized his opportunity. The 1990s were the mirror image of the 1980s. Two recessions and a stock market bubble have impacted the company. As media competition heated up, Mr. Eisner and Disney were caught standing still. ABC's problems were masked by the success of *Who Wants to Be a Millionaire*, while high production costs and quality issues dragged down the performance of the Studio Entertainment division. The Consumer Products division continued its steady slide as management was distracted by the Capital Cities/ABC acquisition and efforts to launch Disney's Internet initiative, Go.Com. The September 11, 2001 tragedy and the dramatic slowdown in economic growth capped the perfect storm. Nonetheless, Mr. Eisner and Disney are in the midst of righting the ship. New management has been installed at ABC and Consumer Products. Specifically, Susan Lyne at ABC is aggressively pursuing new initiatives and fresh programming and

Andy Mooney at Consumer Products is utilizing his strong retail background from Nike to focus the division's brand extension efforts. Studio Entertainment has also become more budget and profit conscious, as evidenced by the success of *Lilo & Stitch,* which exemplifies the company's effort to limit the number of big budget films it produces. The pieces are in place for a turnaround at Disney.

The Disney Board of Directors has been criticized as being too close to Mr. Eisner and not exercising enough diligence in its oversight role. In fact, the Board's independence has recently come under additional scrutiny in light of information filed in the company's latest 10-Q that Disney employed relatives of four Board members. Corporate governance standards recently recommended by the NYSE state that a director is not considered independent if an immediate family member has worked for the company within the past five years. It should be noted, however, that these issues have come to light as a result of Mr. Eisner soliciting the services of Mr. Ira M. Millstein, senior partner in the New York law firm of Weil, Gotshal, & Manges, to review Disney's corporate governance practices in April 2002. Thus far, since employing the services of Mr. Millstein and his firm, the company has instituted new independence standards with key committees restricted to independent directors. The Board is also pushing for reporting transparency and the implementation of all Board recommendations on a timely basis. The revelations in the 10-Q highlight the fact that the company is making progress in assessing the governance procedures. The Board will be meeting in late September of this year to further discuss its own structure and the governance issues.

Stung by the recent performance of the stock, the Board has also become more proactive in its scrutiny of senior management. In 2001 they withheld senior management's bonuses due to the company's poor performance. In addition, three Board members, Stanley Gold, the vice chairman of Disney; Roy Disney; and Thomas Murphy, the former Chairman of Capital Cities/ABC, have expressed their dismay over Mr. Eisner's performance. While Mr. Eisner's ouster in not imminent, the Board finally seems to be exercising some independence. We are optimistic that its initiatives in conjunction with Mr. Eisner's actions will translate into positive results.

QUANTITATIVE APPRAISAL

4. **Sales/Revenue Growth—Pass** Disney's revenues are expected to decline 5 percent in 2002 as a slowing economy and the lingering effects of the September 11, 2001 tragedy impact tourism. However, longer term, Disney's revenues are forecasted to grow 6 to 7 percent, driven principally by the rebound in advertising spending and consumer spending. Approximately 88 percent of the company's revenues are tied to advertising spending and consumer spending. The remaining 12 percent can be characterized as subscription revenues derived mainly from the company's cable channels through their carriage agreements with the cable MSOs.

The lynchpin of the revenue growth forecast is ABC. A better-than-anticipated turnaround at ABC would lift the long-term sales growth forecast for Disney. Broadcasting revenues are anticipated to decline 8 percent this year in contrast to Viacom's Broadcast Network division, which is expected to post a much more modest decline of 2 percent. The company has become more focused on profitable top-line growth than its current results might indicate, however. Longer term, this should translate into revenue growth that is sustainable in the conservative 6 to 7 percent range.

5. **Operating Margins—Pass** Disney's operating margins have declined from 16.8 percent in 2000 to the forecast 10.6 percent in 2002. However, the company in late 2000 to early 2001 initiated a broad cost rationalization plan that should take well over $1 billion out of the company's cost structure. Outside of the slowdown in ad spending and ratings issues at ABC, big budget action films have been the next largest drain on profits. Disney is limiting the number of big budget films it produces and capping its risk on the ones it does produce.

   Animation has also contributed to the problem. *The Lion King*, the huge 1994 hit, cost only $50 million to produce but generated over $1 billion in profits. Since *The Lion King*, recent production costs of animated films have soared, with the production cost of 1999's *Tarzan* reaching a staggering $150 million. However, a turnaround seems at hand as evidenced by Disney's latest animation hit, *Lilo & Stitch*, which was produced for only $80 million. In contrast to the 573 artists who created *Tarzan*, *Lilo & Stitch* was produced with only 208 artists—without sacrificing quality.

   Margins should recover to the 2000 level by 2005. A recovering economy and a rehabilitated ABC will be the primary drivers. Improving broadcasting margins alone will provide one-third of the lift to overall margins should ABC post even a modest recovery. In the interim, as it awaits a recovery in the economy, the company is maintaining its vigil on costs without sacrificing service or quality.

6. **Relative P/E—Pass** The company's current P/E relative to the S&P 500 and based on the consensus 2003 earnings estimate of $0.73 is 1.25 times. On average, the company has traded at 1.50 times the market, with a peak relative multiple of 1.87 times in 1997. The company's current austerity measures in response to the economic slowdown and the restructuring initiatives in

place at ABC, Studio Entertainment, and Consumer Products should accelerate earnings growth once the economy recovers. A better-than-expected economic growth scenario could produce earnings of $1.10 to $1.20 as early as 2004. Thus, we believe there is substantial room for multiple expansions if the company can continue to deliver sound operating results ahead of a recovery in the economy.

7. **Positive Free Cash Flow—Pass** Disney is expected to generate cash flow after investments of −$3.6 billion in fiscal 2002. This is due in large part to the acquisition of Fox Family Worldwide in 2001 for $5.3 billion. Cash flow after investments peaked in 2000 at $2.7 billion. Operating cash flow (OCF) peaked in 2000 at $3.8 billion with OCF expected to trough in fiscal 2002 at $2.2 billion. Though the company is only expected to produce EPS for fiscal 2002 of $0.56, OCF per share will be significantly higher at $1.05 per share. Operating cash flow and free cash flow should trend up with a recovery in the economy and improved operating performance. Free cash flow growth should outpace earnings per share growth for the next several years as the company rationalizes its investments in Theme Parks and Film and Television production costs. This should set the stage for either the retirement of debt or share repurchases.

8. **Dividend Coverage and Growth—Pass** After the recent sharp drop in the stock price, Disney now sports a dividend yield of 1.43 percent. The payout ratio on this year's depressed earnings per share estimate of $0.56 is a healthy 38 percent. Though earnings growth has decelerated over the past several years, Disney's dividend has grown at a rate of 5.4 percent over the past five years. That said, the dividend has remained flat at $0.21 per share since 1999. However, the investment case for Disney is not contingent on the dividend yield or the rate of dividend growth. Investors would be happier to see

the company deleveraging its balance sheet or repurchasing shares at the current stock price rather than increasing the dividend. In fact, Disney is the only media company that pays a dividend.

9. **Asset Turnover—Fail** Asset turns, having peaked in 1995 at 0.88, have been declining as capital expenditures have outpaced revenue growth and the Capital Cities/ABC acquisition has produced mixed results. From 1997 to 2001, net Property Plant and Equipment (PP&E) has increased 36 percent, while sales have increased only 12.4 percent. Declining capital expenditures, an increased focus on profitability, and an improving economy should conservatively increase turns to the 0.60 level by 2005. This would be in line with our forecasting sales growth of 6 percent and earnings of $1.22. While the projection for 2005 is above current levels, it is still well below the peak and depends heavily on the turnaround at ABC. Therefore, Disney fails on this metric.

10. **Investment in Business/ROIC—Fail** Disney's return on capital for the last twelve months was 3.9 percent, well below the company's 7.4 percent cost of capital. The company's focus on reducing debt and increasing profitability should improve returns, particularly as operating margins are expected to rebound to 16 percent from the current 10 percent by 2005. The operating leverage of the business should at a minimum help the company return to generating profits consistent with 1997's 8.3 percent ROIC. If the company is successful in its turnaround efforts and the economy cooperates, operating income growth will outpace revenue growth by a factor of 3. The company's current poor showing, however, results in it failing this factor.

11. **Equity Leverage—Fail** The leverage ratio has remained fairly stable at 2.1 for the last five years; however,

retained earnings have only managed to grow at an annualized rate of 6 percent during this time frame. The last three years in fact have seen no growth in retained earnings. The company should be commended for focusing on its core business and not falling prey to the temptation of acquiring cable assets following the AOL-Time Warner merger. That said, since the Capital Cities/ABC merger in 1996, assets have risen threefold while earnings per share have shown very little growth. The equity market capitalization of the company since the deal was announced has shrunk from $47 billion to $29 billion. Granted, a portion of the current decline is reflective of the current economic environment. However, as previously stated, the poor performance is also attributable to neglect at several key divisions.

12. **Financial Risk—Pass** Michael Eisner, Chairman & CEO, and Tom Staggs, CFO, have certified Disney's financial statements.

Disney's long-term debt has ballooned to $14.7 billion from $8.9 billion in June 2001. The Fox Family acquisition was funded with $2.9 billion of long-term borrowings in addition to the assumption of $2.3 billion in debt. Disney's current debt/equity ratio is 50 percent, up from 21 percent in 1997.

Post Disney's Fiscal Third Quarter 2002 results, S&P placed Disney's long-term credit rating of A− on watch for possible downgrade. More than likely, Disney's long-term debt will be downgraded to BBB+. The weakness in the Theme Parks segment, aided by the uncertainty of the economic recovery, will more than likely leave Disney short of S&P's 2.5 times Debt/EBITDA requirement. Disney does not have downgrade triggers associated with any of its debt; however, a downgrade would increase future borrowing cost and alter its EBITDA/Interest ratio. Disney's current EBITDA/Interest ratio of

7.4 times does leave the company with enough cushion to cover interest expenses. However, interest expense is expected to increase 50 percent in 2003 to $726 million from the current $482 million. If the economic environment remains stagnant, the coverage ratio could conceivably deteriorate to 4.9 times in 2003. The good news is that Disney is only required to maintain an EBITDA/Interest ratio of 3.0 times on the long-term portion (50 percent) of its commercial paper backstop.

Disney's off-balance sheet liabilities are:

I Future minimum lease payments of $1.8 billion for noncancelable operating leases.

I A make-good termination payment to the lessor of the Disneyland Paris Theme Park assets should Euro Disney choose not to exercise the option to assume the terms of the lease Disney SNC (a Disney affiliate) negotiated. Disney SNC then can either purchase the assets, continue to lease the assets, or terminate the lease, in which case Disney SNC would make a termination payment to the lessor equal to 75 percent of the lessor's then-outstanding debt related to the Theme Park assets, estimated to be $1.1 billion. The lease agreement expires in 2006.

I The company's equity contribution to Hong Kong Disneyland over the next five years is $315 million with Disney's equity stake set at 43 percent.

We believe Disney's debt is manageable, though the company has placed a high priority on reducing long-term debt. EBITDA is more than sufficient to cover interest expense; however, we would become more cautious on the stock should EBITDA deteriorate and/or the company fail to reduce debt.

Harshal Shah, CFA
August 12, 2002

INDEX

ABC Entertainment, 204
ABC Family, 203
ABC Television Network, 113, 114, 203, 208
Absolute measures, importance of relative measures versus, 42
Absolute yield, 7
Accounting scandals, 63
Adelphia Communications, 63
Advanced portfolio analysis, 25
Allen, Marty, 13
Amazon, 37
American Electric Power, 31–32
American Home Products. *See* Wyeth
Amgen, 34, 149–150
AOL, 37
AOL Time Warner, 63, 141, 211
Aramis, 171
Asset-liability management in banking sector analysis, 82–83
Asset quality in banking sector analysis, 82
Assets-to-margin ratio, 65
Asset turnover, 72–73
 for EMC, 193–194
 for Estee Lauder, 177
 for Walt Disney, 210
AT&T, 35, 142
Automatic sell, 139
Aveda, 109
Average-in approach, 136
Avon, 175

Baker, Russell, 156
Banking sector analysis, 80–83
 asset-liability management in, 82–83
 asset quality in, 82
 capital adequacy in, 83
 liquidity/funding mix in, 81–82
 overhead/efficiency in, 81

Bank of California, 22, 23
Bank stocks/financials
 Marsh & McLennan as, 98–100
 Wells Fargo as, 97–98
Bath & Body, 121
Bear market
 current, 161
 of 1973-1974, 17, 21
Bell Atlantic, 101
Bell Labs, 142
Bernstein, Peter, 130
Best, Alfred, 14, 15–16
Beverage firms, 6
Biotech companies, 34, 149
Board of directors, 39. *See also* Top management
 independence and relevance of, 58–59
 problematic, 59–60
Bobbi Brown, 178
Book value, 17
Brady, Nicholas, 60
Bristol-Myers Squibb, 106
Buena Vista Television, 203
Buffett, Warren, 14, 17, 21, 85, 147–148, 163
Buggy whip factor, 53
 for EMC, 182–184
 for Estee Lauder, 170
 for Walt Disney, 198–199
Bull market, 17, 21, 35, 161
Business finance, 16–17

Cadbury Schweppes, 55, 148
Calpine, 64, 78
Capacity swaps, 50n
Cap-ex trends, 74–75
Capital adequacy in banking sector analysis, 82–83
Capital Cities/ABC, 204, 206, 210, 211

Cash flow, positive free, 68–70, 176–177, 192–193, 209
Cellular technology, 35
Centera, 186–187, 190
Chevron, 24, 72
Chrysler, 55
Cisco Systems, 119–120, 158, 159
Citigroup, 155–156
Classic valuation models, 8–9
Client relationship management (CRM), 183, 195n
Clinique, 109, 171
Clinique Laboratories, 172
Clinton, Hillary, 157
Coca-Cola, 17, 27, 29, 147–148, 150, 163
    Relative Dividend Yield for, 27, 28
Colgate, 55
Collins, Jim, 57
Columbia Pictures, 148
Companies
    growth rates and catalysts, 62
    selecting only best, 132
Compaq, 34
Competitive position, 62–63
Compound annual growth rate (CAGR), 182, 195n
Compustat, 48
Concentration, 130–132
Constituencies, 29, 157–161
Consumer stocks, 29
    Gillette as, 93–95
    Kimberly-Clark as, 95–97
Coolidge, Calvin, 154
Corporate boards, 17. See also Top management
    dividend policy for, 18, 23–24
Covariance of return, 133–135
Coverage ratio, trend analysis of, 77
Credit ratings, 78–79
Cuenco, Joseph, 179
Current yield, 71
Cyclical earnings, 39

Data, availability of, 162
Data General, 189, 193
Days of sales outstanding, 192–193
Debt/equity ratio, 77
DeDora, Noel, 39, 43, 51
Defense stocks, 1, 146–147
Dell Computers, 34
Deregulation, 6

DeSimone, Mr., 92
Disney. See Walt Disney
Disney, Roy, 207
Disney Channel, 203
Diversification, 130
Dividend coverage and growth, 70–72, 90
    for Estee Lauder, 177
    for Walt Disney, 210
Dividend-driven valuation models, 10, 11
Dividend-paying companies, 23–24
Dividend-paying cultures, 23, 28
Dividend policy, 16–17, 23
    benefits of stable, 24
    reliability of, 23
Dividends
    changes in role of, 18
    companies paying versus companies not paying, 33–34
    growth rate of, 71–72
    payment of, 4–5
Dividend yield, 34–35
Dodd, David, 4, 5–6, 13, 162
Donna Karan, 171
Dotcom valuations, 156
Dow Jones Industrial Average (DJIA), 9–10, 167
    shift in composition of, 34
Drug stocks. See Pharmaceutical stocks

Earnings, 39
    cyclical, 39
    operating, 39–40
    relationship of sales to, 40, 42
Earnings growth, 75
Earnings leverage, 73
Earnings restatement, 50n
Eastman Kodak, 70, 79–80
Eisner, Michael, 205–206, 207, 211
Electric utilities industry, 71
Electronic Data Systems Corporation, 125–128
Elizabeth Arden, 175
EMC, 73, 115–116
    twelve fundamental factor analysis of, 181–195
Enron, 50n, 63, 64, 77, 106
Equity leverage, 75–77
    for EMC, 194–195
    for Estee Lauder, 178
    for Walt Disney, 211
ESPN, 203, 204

Estee Lauder, 108–110, 143
  twelve fundamental factor analysis of, 169–179
Express, 121
Exxon Mobil, 86–87

Fallen angels, 38, 143, 163
  Coca-Cola as, 17, 27, 28, 29, 147–148, 150, 163
  General Electric as, 90–91
  Home Depot as, 41, 116–117
  Relative Dividend Yield chartsfor, 28
  3M as, 91–93
  transformation of former, 128
FASB 76, 142
Fidelity, 25
Financial companies, relationship between information technology and, 135
Financial reporting, fairness and accuracy in, 15
Financial risk, 77–79
  for EMC, 195
  for Estee Lauder, 178–179
  for Walt Disney, 211–213
Financial services industry, 1980s trends in, 25
The Financial World, 14–15
Fisher, Phillip, 129
Foley, Tom, 59–60
Food processing firms, 6
Fox Family Worldwide, 209, 211
Franchise or niche value in qualitative appraisal, 53–57, 68
  for EMC, 184–187
  for Estee Lauder, 170–171
  increase in, 56
  for Walt Disney, 199–205
Fraud, 14
Fremont Investment Advisors (FIA), 165
Fremont New Era Value Fund, 151
Friedman, Milton, 162
Fundamental stock analysis, 16
Fund managers, value investing for, 11
Fund nomenclature, 10

Gabelli, Mario, 14
Gaghan, Chris, 188
Genentech, 34, 150
General Electric, 90–91, 150, 163
Generally accepted accounting principles (GAAP), 39

General Motors, 125
Gillette, 54, 55, 93–95
Gillette, King, 93
Glaxo-Wellcome, 88
Goizueta, Robert, 148
Gold, Stanley, 207
Good to Great (Collins), 57, 83n, 104n
Goodwill, 76, 141, 178
Graham, Benjamin, 4, 5–6, 13, 16, 18, 162
Graham and Dodd model, 4–5
  absolute dividend criteria of, 7
  evaluation of, 7
Growth-oriented economy, 7–8, 10
Growth stock status, 27
Grubman, Jack, 158
GTE, 35
Guenther, Louis, 14–15

Hawley, Michael, 94
HBO, 204
Health care industry, 157
Health care stocks, 1, 34–35
Hedge funds, 137–138
Heinz, 59–60, 102–104
Hewlett-Packard, 46, 123–125, 184, 185, 191
Historical growth rates, 61
Hitachi, 184, 185, 189
Hoechst, 92
Home Depot, 41, 116–117
Honeywell, 90

IBM, 17, 34, 56, 184, 185, 186, 189, 191, 192
Icahn, Carl, 17
I. Magnin, 171
Income equity collective funds, 23
Industry growth rate, 62
Industry margins, operating margins relative to, 64–65
Inflation, 7, 17
Information technology, relationship between financial companies and, 135
Initial public offerings (IPOs), 106
Insurance stocks, 15
Intel, 9–10, 34, 35, 40, 56, 107–108, 158, 160
The Intelligent Investor (Graham), 18
Interbrand Corp., 55
International Paper, 74
Internet, benefits of, 37

Intrinsic value of stocks, 15, 16
Investment climate, technological factors influencing, 25
Investment discipline, 2–4
    need for, 21
    Relative Dividend Yield as, 7–8
    revising, 4
Investment in business. *See* Return on Invested Capital (ROIC)
Investment managers, critical lessons learned as, 153–163
Ivester, Douglas, 148

JC Penny, 53, 80
Johnson, William, 103–104
Johnson & Johnson, 29, 30–31, 47, 150
Jordan, Michael, 54, 118

Kelly, Kevin, 36
Killer applications, 183
Kilts, James, 94
Kimberly-Clark, 95–97, 104*n*
Kozlowski, Dennis, 63

La Mer, 178
Lane Bryant, 121
Langhammer, Fred, 172
Large cap portfolio managers, problems faced by, 131–132
Large cap stocks, 44
Lauder, Estee, 171. *See also* Estee Lauder
Lauder, Leonard A., 172
Lauder, Ronald S., 172
Law of increasing returns, 36
Lerner New York, 121
Life insurance companies, 6
The Limited, 120–121
Limited Brands, 47, 120–123
Lincoln, Abraham, 161
Lipper Analytical Services, 145, 146
Liquidity/funding mix in banking sector analysis, 81–82
Loss of constituency, 29
LTV, 17
Lucent, 142, 143
Lyne, Susan, 204

M.A.C., 109, 178
Management. *See also* Top management
    analysis of strength of depth and culture, 57–58
    compensation plan for, 58

Market share, maintenance of, 55
Market underperformance, 53–54
Market workouts, as investment opportunities, 156–157
Marsh & McLennan, 98–100
McData, 115
MCI, 35
McKesson Corp., 63
McKinsey & Co., 186, 188
McNerney, W. James, Jr., 92–93
Media Networks, 204
Mercedes-Benz, 56
Merged companies, 141–142
Microsoft, 9–10, 34, 35, 110–112
Milken, Mike, 17
Millstein, Ira M., 206
Miramax, 203
Money management, sound, 2–3
Moody's, 78–79
Mooney, Andy, 204, 205
Morgan Stanley, 138
Morningstar, 145, 146
Murphy, Thomas, 207
Mutual funds
    monitoring firms for, 145, 146
    optimal size of portfolio, 130–131
    proliferation of, during 1980s, 10–11

Nabisco, 94
NASDAQ, 167
Net Current Asset Value, 5
Network Appliance, 184, 191
Networked economy, 36–37
Newburger, Henderson and Loeb, 5
New economy, 36, 154
Newell, Roger, 22, 23
The New Era of Wealth (Wesbury), 36, 49*n*
New Era Value composite, 165–167
New Rules for the New Economy (Kelly), 36, 49*n*
Niche value, 68. *See also* Franchise or niche value in qualitative appraisal
Nieman Marcus, 171
Nifty Fifty, 17
Nifty Fifty bull market, 21, 35
Nike, 54, 56, 117–119, 204, 206
Non-farm productivity, 37, 38, 50*n*
NYNEX, 101

Obsolescence, 53
Off-balance sheet financing, 77, 79
Oil stocks, 1, 24
    Exxon Mobil, 86–87

Old economy, 36
Operating cash flow, 209
Operating earnings, 39–40
Operating margins, 64–66, 75–76
    for EMC, 191–192
    for Estee Lauder, 174–175
    relative to industry margins, 64–65
    trend analysis of, 64
    for Walt Disney, 208–209
Oppenheimer, Henry, 5
Option programs, share buy-backs in
    funding, 8
Oracle, 112–113, 158, 159, 163
O'Reilly, Tony, 103–104
Origins, 109
Overhead/efficiency, in banking sector
    analysis, 81
Overvaluation, 27

Payout ratio, 71
Perot, Ross, 125
Perrier, 148
Pharmaceutical stocks, 29, 34–35, 149
    relationship between technology stocks
    and, 134
    Wyeth, 88–89
Pickens, T. Boone, 17
Polaroid, 17, 92
Positive free cash flow, 68–70
    for EMC, 192–193
    for Estee Lauder, 176–177
    for Walt Disney, 209
Prefontaine, Steve, 54
Price, Michael, 14
Price/book (P/B) value ratio, 145
Price-earnings (P/E) ratios, 5, 7
    investor bid up of, 35
    relative, 66–68
Price-to-sales ratios, 42
Pricing power, 54, 56
Procter & Gamble, 96
Productivity, 8, 37
    historical view of U.S., 37–49
    measuring non-farm, 50n
Product obsolescence, 53
Proxy statement, reading, 58
Purchasing power, 54
Putnam, 100

Qualitative appraisal
    buggy whip factor in, 53, 170, 182–184,
    198–199
    franchise or niche value in, 53–57,
    170–171, 184–187, 199–205

top management in, 57–60, 171–173,
    187–189, 205–207
Quantitative appraisal, 61–80
    asset turnover in, 72–73, 177, 193–194, 210
    dividend coverage and growth in, 70–72,
    90, 177, 210
    equity leverage in, 75–77, 178, 194–195, 211
    financial risk in, 77–80, 178–179, 195,
    211–213
    operating margins in, 64–66, 174–175,
    191–192, 208–209
    positive free cash flow in, 68–70, 176–177,
    192–193, 209
    relative price-earnings ratio in, 66–68,
    175–176, 192, 209
    return on invested capital in, 73–75,
    177–178, 194, 210–211
    sales/revenue growth in, 61–63, 173–174,
    189–191, 207–208
Quantitative screens, 16
Qwest, 141, 142

Railroads, 146
RDY. *See* Relative Dividend Yield
Reader's Digest, 60, 65–66, 80
Regional Bell operating companies,
    35, 101
Relative Dividend Yield (RDY), 11, 14, 51,
    146, 165
    building value-driven portfolio
    using, 129
    buy range for, 29
    calculation of, 26–27
    case studies in
        Electronic Data Systems Corporation,
        125–128
        Exxon Mobil, 86–87
        General Electric, 90–91
        Gillette, 93–95
        Heinz, 102–104
        Hewlett-Packard, 123–125
        Kimberly-Clark, 95–97, 104n
        Limited Brands, 120–123
        Marsh & McLennan, 98–100
        3M, 91–93
        Verizon, 101–102
        Wells Fargo, 97–98
        Wyeth, 88–89
    development of, 21–32
    as investment discipline, 7–8, 32, 33
    in portfolio, 132–133
    thresholds for buy and sell ranges, 28
    as valuation benchmark, 7–8, 23, 39

*Relative Dividend Yield: Common Stock
    Investing for Income and Appreciation*
    (Spare and Tengler), 26, 32*n*
Relative Dividend Yield charts, 26
    for fallen angels, 28
Relative information, value of, 22
Relative measures, importance of absolute
    measures to, 42
Relative price, 32*n*
Relative price-earnings, 66–68
    for EMC, 192
    for Estee Lauder, 175–176
    for Walt Disney, 209
Relative Price-to-Sales Ratio (RPSR), 14, 43,
    51, 146, 165
    building value-driven portfolio
        using, 129
    case studies for, 14, 51, 105–106
        Cisco Systems, 119–120
        Electronic Data Systems Corporation,
        125–128
        EMC, 115–116
        Estee Lauder, 108–110
        Hewlett-Packard, 123–125
        Home Depot, 116–117
        Intel, 107–108
        Limited Brands, 120–123
        Microsoft, 110–112
        Nike, 117–119
        Oracle, 112–113
        Walt Disney Company, 113–115
    mechanics of, 48–49
    non-applicability, 48
    in portfolio, 132–133
    technology bubble and, 106
    testing methodology of, 45–48
    use of, to evaluate stocks of all market
        caps, 43–44
Relative Value Discipline (RVD), 11, 14, 151,
    165
Relative value investing, 42
Research and development, 75
Retail market, bifurcation into distinct
    segments, 53
Retained earnings, 16
Return on invested capital (ROIC), 36, 73–75
    for EMC, 194
    for Estee Lauder, 177–178
    for Walt Disney, 210–211
Revlon, 175
Risk, 29
    value investing and, 10

Rogers, Will, 51, 153
ROIC. *See* Return on invested capital (ROIC)
Roosevelt, Theodore, 162
Rose, Leonard, 51
Round trip contracts, 50*n*
RPSR. *See* Relative Price-to-Sales Ratio
    (RPSR)
Rukeyser, Louis, 1
Russell 1000 Growth, 3
Russell 1000 Index, 138
Russell 1000 Value Index, 3, 167

Saks, 171
Sales, 40
    relationship of, versus earnings, 40, 42
    as valuation indicator, 45
Sales contact management (SCM),
    183, 195*n*
Sales/revenue growth, 61–63
    for EMC, 189–191
    for Estee Lauder, 173–174
    for Walt Disney, 207–208
Sales-to-margin ratio, 65
Samuelson, Paul A., 154
Sanders, Wayne, 96
S&P 500, 9, 33, 43, 56, 78–79, 98
    historical price-to-sales ratio of, 43
S&P Barra Growth, 143, 151
S&P Barra Value Indices, 143, 151
S&P 500 Growth Index, 145
S&P 500 Index, 91, 167
    shift in composition of, 34
Scott Paper, 96
Sears, 53
Sector weightings, 135–136
Security Analysis (Graham and Dodd), 4,
    13, 14, 16, 18
Selling, General, and Administrative figures,
    62
Service obsolescence, 53
Shah, Harshal, 195, 213
Share buy-backs, 8
Shareholders' equity, 83
Shareholder value, 58
Skilling, Jeffrey, 64
Small cap stocks, 43
Smith Kline Beecham, 88
Soap Net, 203
S&P 500, 145
Spare, Tony, 22, 23, 26
Spitzer, Eliot, 158
Sprint, 35

Staggs, Tom, 211
Stevenson, Adlai, 33
Stock
  historical price-to-sales ratio of, 43
  impact of technology on analysis of, 21–22
  intrinsic value of, 15, 16
  junk, 42
  terminally cheap, 48, 51, 71, 100–104
Stock market, shift in sector concentration
    in, 8–9
Stock options, 58
Stock portfolio, 11
  advanced analysis of, 25
  best companies in, 132
  concentration of stocks in, 130–132
  covariance in, 133–135
  management tools for, 25
  optimal size of, 130–131
  RDY stocks in, 132–133
  RPSR stocks in, 132–133
  weightings/diversification, 135–141
Stop-loss orders, 139, 142, 161
Sun Microsystems, 184, 185, 186, 191, 193
Survivorship bias, 45, 50n

Takeovers, 7
Target, 53
Technology, impact of, on stock analysis,
    21–22
Technology bubble, 36
  Relative Price-to-Sales Ratio and, 106
Technology stocks
  relationship between pharmaceutical
    stocks and, 134
  rise of, 34
Telecommunications, 35, 50n
Terminally cheap stocks, 48, 51, 71, 100
  Heinz as, 102–104
  Verizon as, 101–102
3M, 91–93
Time Warner Cable, 114
Time-weighted total returns, 165, 167
Top-line growth, 40
Top management, 39, 57–60
  for EMC, 187–189
  for Estee Lauder, 171–173
  for Walt Disney, 205–207
Total cost of ownership, 184
Touchstone Television, 203
Trend analysis
  of coverage ratio, 77
  of operating margins, 64

  of return on invested capital, 74
  of working capital turnover, 69
Triggers, 139–141
Tucci, Joe, 186, 188
Turning points, 157–161
Twelve Fundamental Factors, 51–83, 129
  analysis of EMC by, 181–195
  analysis of Estee Lauder by,
    169–179
  analysis of Walt Disney by, 197–213
  asset turnover in, 72–73, 177, 193–194, 210
  banking sector and, 80–83
  buggy whip factor in, 53, 170, 182–184,
    198–199
  case study of Eastman Kodak, 70, 79–80
  case study of *Reader's Digest*, 65–66
  dividend coverage and growth in, 70–72,
    90, 177, 210
  equity leverage in, 75–77, 178, 194–195,
    211
  in era of accounting scandals, 63–64
  financial risk in, 77–80, 178–179, 195,
    211–213
  franchise or niche value in, 53–57,
    170–171, 184–187, 199–205
  operating margins in, 64–66, 174–175,
    191–192, 208–209
  positive free cash flow in, 68–70, 176–177,
    192–193, 209
  relative price-earnings ratio in, 66–68,
    175–176, 192, 209
  return on invested capital in, 73–75,
    177–178, 194, 210–211
  sales/revenue growth in, 61–63, 173–174,
    189–191, 207–208
  top management in, 57–60, 171–173,
    187–189, 205–207
Tyco International, 63

Undervaluation, 27
Undervalued stocks
  as good value, 16
  need for investment discipline to identify,
    38–39
Union Bank of California, 33
Upgrade/downgrade-after-the-fact condition,
    160–161
US West, 141

Value-driven portfolio, constructing,
    129–143
Value fund managers, 8

Value hedge funds, 8
Value investing
   basis for, 2
   changes in concept of, 16
   characteristics of, 10
   defined, 14
   forced change in fundamentals of, 17–18
   for fund managers, 11
   as method for selecting stock, 4
   potential extensions of, 8–10
   risk and, 10
   rule set for, 4, 5
   in today's market, 145–151
Value investors, 1, 2
   challenge of building diversified
      portfolios, 8
   exclusion of, from innovative sectors of
      market, 9–10
Value judgments, 162
Value-oriented investors, challenge
      for, 38
Verizon, 101–102
Viacom, 208
Victoria's Secret, 121

Wall Street, tendency to extrapolate recent
      events, 37
Wal-Mart, 53
Walt Disney, 113–115
   twelve fundamental factor analysis of,
      197–213
Walt Disney Television, 203
The Washington Post, 17
Welch, Jack, 90
Wells Fargo, 57–58, 97–98
Wesbury, Brian, 36
Western Electric, 142
Weyerhaeuser, 74
Wilde, Oscar, 157
Woods, Tiger, 54, 118
Working capital turnover, 192–193
   trend analysis of, 69
WorldCom, 50n, 63, 158
Write-offs history, 76
Wyeth, 88–89

Xerox, 17, 63, 80

Yields, 29